GAY/LESBIAN
LIBERATION

A Biblical Perspective

GAY/LESBIAN LIBERATION

A Biblical Perspective

GEORGE R. EDWARDS

The Pilgrim Press
New York

The scripture quotations in this book, unless otherwise indicated, are
from the *Revised Standard Version of the Bible,* copyright 1946, 1952,
1957, and © 1971, 1973 by the Division of Christian Education,
National Council of Churches, and are used by permission. Excerpts
marked NEB are from *The New English Bible,* © The Delegates of the
Oxford University Press and the Syndics of the Cambridge University
Press 1961, 1970, and are used by permission.

Library of Congress Cataloging in Publication Data

Edwards, George R., 1920–
   Gay/lesbian liberation.

   Bibliography: p. 130.
   Includes index.
     1. Homosexuality—Religious aspects—Christianity.
   2. Homosexuality—Biblical teaching.
   3. Liberation theology.   I. Title.
   BR115.H6E33   1984   261.8'35766   84-1143
   ISBN 0-8298-0725-X (pbk.)

2d printing, 1986

The Pilgrim Press, 132 West 31 Street, New York, NY 10001

CONTENTS

FOREWORD

This is a blockbuster of a book. Which is saying a good bit for a book that is first and foremost a work in theology, and the theology of Paul at that! Engrossingly lucid and honest, it states the case for human sexuality as an authentic and guiltless expression of the love of God.

More precisely it is about the reality of homosexual love, but it elucidates that topic with constant reference to heterosexual love. In essence, the author lets us see how all the perversions and glories of human love imaginable fall within both modes of human loving. There is no salvation or damnation per se either in heterosexual coupling or in homosexual coupling. Theologically framed, in the loving embrace of God in Christ there is neither homosexual nor heterosexual, just as there is neither Jew nor Greek, slave nor free, male nor female.

This insistent extension of *agapē* to homosexuality should not be misconstrued for mushy thinking or sentimental condescension. Before ascending to the theological summit, the author traverses extensive ground that is ingredient to his final destination. Edwards helps us to see homosexuals in their great variety as actual people who inhabit and share our cultural space. Stereotypes and prejudices—as well as distorted biblical interpretations wrested from context—fall in rows before the finely honed blade of this analyst of one of the last great unconfronted phobias of our culture.

As I perceive the book, its energy and passion stem from a shocking personal experience of the author related on pages 119–20. But that is only the book's point of ignition. Its total effect is that of a refiner's fire. This is achieved through the author's undeterred quest for the roots of homophobia so wild and bitter that it could erupt in the bloody beating of a gay just for being "a god damned queer" and in the consignment of tens of thousands of homosexuals to death in Nazi Germany. While most heterosexuals would not admit to wanting to beat or kill "perverts," why have homosexuals been cast as pariahs, stigmatized as sick or sinful, condemned of God, "set up" for beatings and killings?

In the course of his inquiry, Edwards not only plumbs the depths of the meaning of the grace and love of God for us humans, but he painstakingly reviews and reconstructs the interpretation of those relatively few biblical texts on homosexuality. He well understands that it is these texts—as traditionally appropriated—that have reinforced and justified the cruel repression of homosexuals in Christian societies down to the present moment. The bloodied homosexual whom the author rescued from his "upright" heterosexual assailant was the victim of generations of self-righteous Christian sexual ideology in which heterosexuality was itself grossly deformed by male domination. Insecure and loveless heterosexuals, Christians though they be, understandably fear and hate to see themselves mirrored in loveless homosexuals or surpassed in loving homosexuals. There is then something about our troubled heterosexuality that we think we see in the homosexual and which, if unacknowledged, impels us to repress our feelings within and oppress the homosexual without.

The intellectual and theological power of this book derives from an uncompromising application of liberation hermeneutics which refuses to grant that only certain categories of oppressed peoples are worthy of liberation. The effect is discomfiting and cleansing in the very best tradition of liberation theology. Here we grasp that liberation theology is not just for poor Latin Americans but takes its own form for psychosocially constricted North Americans whose material plenty is unmatched by a mature sexuality. In Edwards' hermeneutic there are no cheap points gained by twisting and stretching biblical texts so that they say what the author wants to claim about homosexuality. Instead, he reminds us of the largely unnoted depth dimension in biblical interpretation, namely, the circumstances and perspectives of the interpreter. If the mind of the interpreter is crammed with ignorance and defensiveness about homosexuality, the biblical texts on homosexuality will be fantasized to suit the interpreter's worst imaginings.

Since our culture is saturated with a deeply ignorant homophobia, Edwards accepts the task of motivating his readers to want to overcome ignorance concerning all aspects of homosexuality. As a biblical scholar, he shoulders a good part of this demystifying project. By the time we reach the biblical texts, it does not surprise us to find that they say both *less* and *more*, and often *entirely other*, than we once thought. Who would have guessed, for example, that the horrendous "sodomy" of Genesis 19 is, more than anything else, an offshoot of hostile heterosexuality in which defeated or subordinate males are humiliated by being treated like women?

Finally, Edwards understands that the fight for the social dignity of loving homosexuality is a political fight. He informs us of the little-known Stonewall Rebellion in New York City in 1969 when homosexuals first fought back collectively and openly against their oppression. The title of the book is important at this juncture. Instead of the relatively mild "homosexual freedom," Edwards has chosen the more political and militant "gay/lesbian liberation." It is a Christian manifesto, a concerted "fightback" for the possibility and reality of same-sex love fully the equal of opposite-sex love.

No reader is likely to feel neutral about this call to gay/lesbian liberation on Christian foundations. Because of the self-reflective quality of Edwards' presentation, however, it is not easy to come away from the book simply saying "yes" or "no" to his argument. In order to understand what the author is saying, one is compelled to look so closely at one's own sexuality and theology that one's view of homosexuality in Christian context is likely from then on to be informed by new insights about one's sexual self and new sensibilities about the culture and politics of sexuality in this society. In particular, the author's notion of "transgenital awareness" shows vividly how gay liberation is in continuity with the struggle to overthrow all those fear-ridden stereotypes that block the way to mature personhood and a just society.

> *Transgenital awareness* attempts to place sexuality in appropriate relationship to the total moral task of liberating love. Men and women do not live by sex alone. To designate someone "a homosexual" usually means to give that person a genital identity to which everything else is subordinate. Gay/lesbian liberation is the overcoming of this genital stereotype, establishing personhood beyond the confines of sexual functions. At stake in transgenital awareness is the placing of sexuality in a total spectrum of moral challenges pertinent to human liberation and impinging on sexuality in such a way that its growth toward completeness, its history, is without them stunted [p. 123].

I found this book to be one of those occasional "small" books so well written, so seamless in argument, so insistent on making one think for oneself against the cultural tide, that one regrets to see them end. One wishes for more. In this case, the "more" we are given is an imperative to think through and live out the author's central thesis that "*agapē* love morally informs human sexuality and mediates to it the experience of liberation [p. 107]."

Norman K. Gottwald

PREFACE

By the end of 1983 it became redundant to speak of living in illiberal times. Some thirty-five years of teaching have made it clear to me that science, theology, and pedagogy itself have no inherent immunity to transcendent social and political forces that shape human destiny. The fantasy of factuality and historical objectivity give to education a compounded illusion of virtue even while producing results by no means virtuous.

One sign of our times is that evangelical conservatism, by abbreviating its name to the one word evangelical, seeks to harness scripture to forms of religious belief and social practice essentially at variance with human freedom. This captivity of scripture will not be easily ended. Under the desire to shorten its duration, my focus eventually shifted from a study of homosexuality to the theme of lesbian and gay liberation. Mere slogans of liberation, however, do not guarantee that an unwanted bondage has been broken; they may be the prelude to a new and more inhuman oppression.

The assertion "God says," when applied to any interpretation of a biblical text (particularly texts that treat erotic expression), invites the immediate suspicion that the speaker is either a literalist, or is seeking to reinforce an understanding against which objections of increasing weight are shifting the balance toward a new understanding. There is indeed an unmistakable arrogance in anyone who takes up the phrase "God says" simply because the placing of divine sanction on any human utterance obscures God's hiddenness and ultimacy. In the face of this arrogance the things that are not are chosen by God to bring down the things that are.

It would be fortunate if counterauthority could assure us that its own version of "God says" provides the heavenly guidance that we seek as remedy for an uncertain existence and a history strewn with the wreckage of fallen establishments. But such an assurance should not be pretended.

In the pages that follow the countercultural stone (Daniel 2) is hurled at the great image. However tempered by the awareness of one's own imperfect knowledge, there is an assured boasting in the assumption that the studied asseverations of learned exegetes and the solemn pronouncements of church councils that have repeatedly, in God's name, anathematized homosexual persons, are in error. If the one who throws the stone must be delivered from the illusion that the stone is one made without human hands, destined to become a great mountain called the kingdom of God, the same self-criticism befits those whose concepts of sexual probity bind heavy burdens on people without extending them the lifting power of one compassionate finger.

This book does not rest on the assumption of homosexual sinlessness any more than on the assumption of heterosexual sinlessness. If in the final analysis the *agapē* of God should come nearer to realization in the erotic experience of some people and alert them to the wider vision of social agape that transcends the burning and all-too-often preoccupying power of human sexuality, the reward of my work will more than surpass the burden of it.

During sabbatic leaves generously provided in 1977 and 1982 by my employer, Louisville Presbyterian Theological Seminary, opportunities were provided for pursuing the study of homosexuality in the Bible that I had begun in 1976. These sabbaticals were spent in Tübingen and Edinburgh, cities that offered excellent study resources and continue to occupy a treasured place in my memory.

As early as 1969 The Pilgrim Press, true to the meaning of its name, published *The Same Sex: An Appraisal of Homosexuality,* edited by Ralph W. Weltge. Thus for a long time Pilgrim editors have shown themselves attentive to a subject of far-reaching biblical and ethical ramifications. With courage and foresight they are providing channels for a discussion that reaches as far into human antiquity as it impacts profoundly on our contemporary social life. My benediction on them is not to charge to their account any misjudgments this book may contain, but to honor in their example the God whose "not yet" rebukes the certitude of a visible power that remains impervious to the things hoped for.

GAY/LESBIAN LIBERATION

A Biblical Perspective

CHAPTER/ONE

Gay/Lesbian Liberation Within Contemporary Theology

Can gay/lesbian liberation claim a rightful place in the struggle for human freedom, or is it an unwanted and unjustifiable intrusion? This is the question posed in these opening pages. Does gay/lesbian liberation belong to the genre of liberation theology understood as a biblically based theology? I will examine in summary form the contributions of contemporary sexology, which must affect the interpretation of biblical texts pertinent to homosexuality.

BIBLICAL INTERPRETATION WITHIN LIBERATION THEOLOGY

In his perceptive monograph *What Is Liberation Theology?*[1] Jorge Lara-Braud traces the "authoritative foundation" of liberation theology to the Second General Conference of Latin American Roman Catholic Bishops, which took place at Medellín, Colombia, in August 1968. Lara-Braud is fully aware that the roots of liberation theology predate 1968. No less does he understand that to cast it in the mold specific to the experience of Latin American Catholicism is to limit unwarrantedly the breadth of applications this theology invites.[2] Medellín is a significant, exemplary instance rather than the definitive statement of the theology of liberation.

To speak of Medellín is to speak of the Peruvian theologian Gustavo Gutiérrez, whose thought significantly shaped the Medellín

---

[1](Atlanta: General Assembly Mission Board, Presbyterian Church in the United States, 1980), p. 9.

[2]For example, through inattention to women's liberation or black liberation as expressed in the theology of North America, Africa, and other continents.

3

materials on justice and peace, particularly as these topics have impact on the politics of development by which industrialized nations have sought to meet the revolution of rising expectations among less-developed societies. In his 1971 book, *A Theology of Liberation,* Gutiérrez summarized his contradistinctions between development and liberation in the following threefold formulation, the third part of which accents the place of biblical sources.

First, *development* obscures the conflictual realities that attend the oppressed/oppressor relationship dominating socioeconomic interchange between poor and wealthy societies or classes within societies, the remedy for which is not development but *liberation.* Second, liberation properly focuses human responsibility and potentiality for the task of personal and collective freedom, so that a new history emerges as freedom emerges. Third, liberation, more than development, "allows for another approach leading to the biblical sources" that depict Christ as liberator from sin, the root of all injustice.[3]

The emphases of Gutiérrez already suggest how liberation theology proposes a new approach to biblical literature. This took particular shape in the 1976 work of Juan Luis Segundo, *The Liberation of Theology,* in which he discussed the "hermeneutic circle."[4] As Segundo acknowledges, the phrase "hermeneutical[5] circle" goes back to a 1925 essay by Rudolf Bultmann entitled "The Problem of a Theological Exegesis of the New Testament."[6] It is important to remember Bultmann's emphasis that a text is not understood without a preunderstanding brought by the interpreter to the text. The very mode of questioning by which the text is understood is determined by this preunderstanding; but preunderstanding cannot remain closed to the text or prejudge the message it conveys.[7] Thus the interpretation is a bipolar movement, a "circle" traversed over

[3]Gustavo Gutiérrez, *A Theology of Liberation,* trans. and ed. Sister Caridad Inda and John Eagelson (Peru, 1971; Maryknoll, NY: Orbis Books, 1973), pp. 36–37.

[4]Juan Luis Segundo, *Liberation of Theology,* trans. John Drury (Maryknoll, NY: Orbis Books, 1976), pp. 7–38.

[5]The longer form of the adjective is used as a matter of preference.

[6]"Das Problem einer theologischen Exegese des Neuen Testaments," *Zwischen den Zeiten* 3 (1925):337–57. This reference is from Walter Schmithals, *An Introduction to the Theology of Rudolf Bultmann,* trans. John Bowden (Minneapolis: Augsburg, 1968), p. 325. My comments on Bultmann are derived from Schmithals' treatment of Bultmann's hermeneutical method, pp. 220–72.

[7]Rudolf Bultmann, "Is Exegesis Without Presuppositions Possible?" *Existence and Faith,* trans. Schubert Ogden (New York: Meridian, 1960), p. 289.

and again, wherein a text impacts and alters the understanding that the questions addressed to it already imply. Closely allied to preunderstanding in Bultmann is his use of "content criticism" *(Sachkritik)*. Using content criticism, one may distinguish between what a text says and what is meant. Although the meaning depends on and arises from the text, all the words and sentences do not equally and invariably serve the subject matter effectively, and they must be refined in the light of it. Martin Luther used content criticism in judging critically both the content of the canon—what "emphasizes Christ"—and what the true canon communicates—salvation by faith alone. The negative result is that some passages obscure rather than clarify the real subject matter. Again, however, the circular movement is operative, because the content that is used to criticize the text arises from it and is rendered valid only by vigorous interchange with it.

Into this formulation of the hermeneutical circle Segundo introduced the notion of ideological suspicion. The word ideology can have both a neutral and a pejorative sense. In the neutral sense ideology refers to any system of ideas or doctrines without reference to their credibility or value. Karl Mannheim brought out the negative aspect of the term by placing it in a political setting:

> Ruling groups can in their thinking become so intensely interest-bound to a situation that they are simply no longer able to see certain facts which would undermine their sense of domination. There is implicit in the word "Ideology" the insight that in certain situations the collective unconscious of certain groups obscures the real condition of society both to itself and others and thereby stabilizes it.[8]

Erich Fromm reinforces the negative meaning of ideology by emphasizing how we need to believe that we are prompted by such humane and constructive impulses as freedom, equality, and fairness. This need leads us to construct a system of ideas (an ideology) that enables us to disguise to ourselves and others our most "immoral and irrational impulses, making them appear as though they were moral and good."[9] Segundo holds that experience brings us to question not only the whole political and social ideology under which we live but our biblical understanding as well. Ideological

[8]Karl Mannheim, *Ideology and Utopia*, trans. L. Wirth and E. Shils (New York: Harcourt, Brace, and World, 1936), p. 40, cited by Robert McAfee Brown, *Theology in a New Key* (Philadelphia: Westminster Press, 1978), p. 79.
[9]Erich Fromm, *May Man Prevail?* (New York: Doubleday, 1961), p. 122.

suspicion thus gives rise to exegetical suspicion—"suspicion that the prevailing interpretation of the Bible has not taken important pieces of data into account."[10]

In designing his own version of the hermeneutical circle Robert McAfee Brown has attempted to remove the blinders that we bring to scripture out of our own ideological conditioning.[11] In describing the process of interpretation Brown sets forth the fundamental ingredients of what is commonly termed historical-critical exegesis:

1. The text (or passage)
2. The historical situation of the text
3. Our interpretation of the text in its situation

To these traditional elements Brown adds aspects of the liberationist hermeneutic:

4. Our own historical situation *as seen by us* . . .
5. Our own historical situation *as seen by others* . . .
6. Our own historical situation as seen by us once we have listened to the others—so that now we see the text in a new way and thus *approach our own historical situation in a newer way still*
7. Our own historical situation as seen by us once we have listened to the others—so that we now see our situation in a new way and thus *approach the text in a new way.*[12]

With this design Brown reflects the fact that discovering the historical meaning of a text in its own time is an indispensable mark of maturity in the learning process, a goal of human knowledge to be abandoned only at the price of ignorance. At the same time he emphasizes in this approach that unexamined presuppositions have to be brought out and corrected, that "historical" exegesis must include present history as well, the history of the interpreter as well as the interpreter's social situation.

My purpose is to show that gay/lesbian liberation—despite its absence from the agenda of discussion in most writing devoted to

[10] Segundo, *Liberation of Theology*, p. 9.
[11] Brown prefers "circulation" for "circle" to avoid the implication of something completed or closed.
[12] Brown, *New Key*, p. 87.

liberation theology[13]—qualifies for a serious role in the growing influence of this theology. In particular, I wish to challenge those time-honored biblical perspectives that exemplify the kind of ideological overgrowth that must be cut away to recover the instrumentality of scripture for the work of human freedom. However, in examining traditional treatments of biblical passages that have served as favorite proof texts of the sexual majority for repressive attitudes, conduct, and laws, I do not wish to present liberation as a simple overthrow of oppressors by oppressed, despite the appropriateness of that language for the actuality of the sexual situation. Rather, I seek to point toward a biblical understanding of human freedom by which sexual sanity may be discovered as God's gift beyond fragmented and prejudiced conceptions of it.

GAY/LESBIAN LIBERATION BELONGS TO THE THEOLOGY OF LIBERATION

Because liberation theology has been so intimately connected with the state of economic exploitation suffered in less-developed countries, it may be said that the inclusion of gay/lesbian liberation in the agenda of liberation theology is a mixture of subjects lacking any essential mutuality. This objection emphasizes the social and psychological stigmatization of homosexuals as over against institutionalized economic deprivation.

It is incorrect to assume that homosexuals as a group are not subject to extensive economic hardship resulting from professional discrimination. The well-known affluent or professionally successful homosexual does not prove the opposite any more than the affluent, successful black proves that blacks as a group are not economically disadvantaged. As employment opportunities declined in the United States, military recruitment among blacks proceeded vigor-

---

[13] In *Liberation Preaching* (Nashville: Abingdon Press, 1980), for example, a valuable application of liberationist insights to biblical homilectics, Justo L. Gonzales and Catherine G. Gonzales have shown how blacks, Chicanos, Asian and native Americans, women (cf. pp. 11, 12, 52, 59), and even the white male preacher (p. 28) can break into the hermeneutical circle with liberating insight by making use of ideological suspicion. The claims of gay/lesbian liberation remain unexpressed, however, except for one footnote (pp. 115f., n. 15, referring to an article in which J.L. Gonzales affirms that "most Christians would object much more strongly to the ordination of a homosexual than they would to that of a wheeler-dealer").

ously and caused the volunteer army to become disproportionately nonwhite. However, exclusion of homosexuals from military employment continued as before.[14] Moreover, the banning of army recruiters by six major university law schools on this account produced a Pentagon threat to deprive those universities of defense contracts.[15] In 1978 "practicing" homosexuals were excluded from ministerial ordination by the General Assembly of the United Presbyterian Church in the USA. In May 1984 The United Methodist Church also ruled against the ordination of homosexual ministers. The infrequent departures from this ban in the Episcopal Church and in the United Church of Christ accentuate the closed-door policy of the major religious communions. This policy occurs at a time when seminary enrollments of females have risen in many Protestant institutions to one-third or one-half the total. It should be remembered in this context that when the Rev. Troy Perry founded the Metropolitan Community Church, in 1968, he had already been deposed from the Pentecostal ministry because he was gay. There has been no positive sign that the National Council of the Churches of Christ would take affirmative action on the membership overture of the Universal Fellowship of the Metropolitan Community Church, despite the fact that such action would not nullify the moral pronouncements that other member denominations might have made on the subject of homosexuality.[16]

Employed homosexuals are constantly in danger of exposure (by blackmail, extortion, or other means) and dismissal. The notion that homosexuals are well-off financially arises largely from the fact that they have historically suffered in silence the sea of misfortunes that has plagued them. Since the Stonewall rebellion of 1969, when gays in New York fought back against police harassment and provided gay/lesbian liberation in the United States with an historical focal point, the story of homosexual oppression has become more accessible.[17]

[14] A gripping account of the personal and economic impact of exclusion from service in the U.S. Navy as well as from civilian employment providing educational services to Navy personnel is recorded by E. Lawrence Gibson in *Get Off My Ship: Ensign Berg vs. the U.S. Navy* (New York: Avon Books, 1978).

[15] Cheryl M. Fields, "Six Universities Could Lose Defense Contracts over Law Schools Bans on Army Recruiters," *The Chronicle of Higher Education* 24 (August 4, 1982):1. The universities are Columbia, Harvard, New York, Wayne State, Yale, and the University of California at Los Angeles.

[16] See J.C. Lyles, "The Unity They Seek," *Christian Century* 100 (1983):539–40.

[17] On the Stonewall rebellion, see Toby Marotta, *The Politics of Homosexuality* (Boston: Houghton Mifflin, 1981), pp. 71–99.

Even if one is unmindful of the economic predicament of homosexuals, the appropriateness of gay/lesbian liberation as a specific case of liberation theology in general is defensible. This arises partly from the fact that there is no official, authorized version of the philosophical premises of liberation theology. Any proposal of a liberationist orthodoxy would be widely criticized—and appropriately so.

To make this reference specific I introduce at this point a brief overview of the work of José Porfirio Miranda, a well-known Mexican liberation theologian who is distinguished for his systematic correlation of biblical exegesis and Marxist economic analysis. The following discussion of Miranda's work should not be construed as wholesale repudiation of liberation theology or of the contribution Miranda has made to it.

In *Marx and the Bible* Miranda begins with the premise that private ownership (of the means of production) is "legalized, institutionalized, civilized, canonized robbery."[18] The distribution of ownership is only the distribution of accumulated income derived from the surplus value of the workers' labor, surplus value being the value of labor in excess of that necessary to produce the consumer goods needed by the workers. From these maxims emerges in our time the central significance of justice as economic justice. This same economic justice informs the biblical doctrine of God and pervasively rules the consciousness of the prophets. The prohibition of the second commandment (against graven images) does not root in the immateriality of God—true as it is—but in the need of human responsiveness to God's justice. Consequently, in all the prophets, knowledge of God means to achieve justice for the poor, expressed characteristically in Jeremiah 22:13–16, which ends:

> Your father ate and drank like you,
> but *he practised justice and right;*
> this is good.
> *He defended the cause of the poor and the needy;*
> this is good
> *Is not this what it means to know me?* It is
> Jahweh who speaks.[19]

From these introductory precepts on economic justice in the prophets, Miranda proceeds in a straight line (with remarkable, if

[18]José Miranda, *Marx and the Bible: A Critique of the Philosophy of Oppression*, trans. John Eagelson (Maryknoll, NY: Orbis Books, 1974), p. 11.
[19]Cited from Miranda, ibid., p. 44, with his italics. Used by permission.

not unflawed, consistency) to bring the theology of Paul under the same thoroughgoing design already laid down in the prophets.[20] In Romans 1:18—3:20 Paul's scathing declamation against gentile, then Jewish, wrongdoing is to be comprehended entirely by the term injustice, which stands as the first entry in the list of vices embraced in Romans 1:29–31. To reinforce the assertion that injustice is the comprehensive title of the entire list, Miranda (pp. 161f.) removes this word *(adikia)* from its initial place in 1:29 to the conclusion of verse 28 and places after it a colon, thereby making the subsequent verses adjunctive explanations of the single term injustice. This verse division and this punctuation are not confirmed by any current edition of the Greek New Testament and obscure the grammatical fact that injustice *(adikia)* is in no way differentiated from the three nouns that follow it. At verse 29 the construction shifts from the instrumental case (in which "injustice" stands) to the genitive ("full of envy, murder," etc.), forsaking the connection with "injustice" and linking back once again to the "them," object of the verb gave up in verse 28.

By this idiosyncratic rendering of Romans 1:28ff., Miranda intends to prove that Paul has no other conception of the justice of God than is plainly laid out in the prophets and the psalter, a justice he has already interpreted in terms of its antithesis, the private ownership of the means of production. Further, the righteousness (or justice) of God, the single theme on which all of Romans is but commentary, is *now* revealed (Romans 3:21) in the cross and resurrection of Jesus. This means that the eschatological rule of God has been actualized, without residue, in Jesus Christ—actualized, that is, in terms of the final judgment against economic injustice, the deliverance of the oppressed poor. "God is revealed only in the implacable 'now' of the moral imperative of justice and love for all. To postpone the kingdom, to postpone the Messiah, is to prevent them from ever being real."[21] So Christians, who for nineteen centuries have dillydallied (with the connivance and consent of ecclesiastical authorities) about the ending of civilization based on legalized exploitation, have falsified the entire biblical message. Paul's repudiation of the law, the epitome of civilization, is so complete that statements against law by Kropotkin, Bakunin, Marx, and Engels pale by comparison.

[20]Ibid., pp. 39–42. For what follows, see especially pp. 109–92.
[21]José Miranda, *Being and the Messiah: The Message of St. John*, trans. John Eagelson (Maryknoll, NY: Orbis Books, 1977), p. 191.

Miranda's interpretation of the prophets, found with frequency among the liberationists, has much to commend it and serves as a necessary corrective against Christian neglect of the Old Testament and the constant tendency of church and synagogue to sweep the questions of economic justice under the rug. It cannot, however, be conceded that Paul's idea of divine righteousness proceeds in lockstep from the prophets, comprehended through a preunderstanding shaped by nineteenth-century Marxism.

Miranda well understands that Romans 5—8, alongside the Galatian letter in particular, expounds what Paul means by the freedom of the one who by faith (in Jesus) is righteous. In Romans and Galatians, Paul goes beyond the *moral* sense of Habakkuk 2:4 ("the just one will live by faithfulness"), making the final clause of Habakkuk not a modifier of the verb will live but attributive to "just one." Hence the *Revised Standard Version* correctly reads (after changing the masculine pronoun) at Romans 1:17, "[the one] who through faith is righteous shall live." Miranda doggedly attempts to make all of Galatians and Romans subservient to the program of economic justice he finds in Romans 1:18—3:20. But this reductionism eclipses the remarkable element characterizing Paul's distinctive emphasis in Romans 5—the justification of the unjust. In his polite foreword to Miranda's *Marx and the Bible*, José María Díez-Alegría has, therefore, voiced a substantial criticism:

> It seems to me that when Paul speaks of the "justice of faith" in contradistinction to the "justice of the law," his point of view is less directly and exclusively "political" than Miranda makes it. . . . Perhaps Miranda takes for granted a pure and simple continuity between the prophetic outlook of the Old Testament and the outlook of the New Testament.[22]

Despite Miranda's commendable concern to restore the prophetic moral quality of biblical justice, Paul stubbornly refuses to dilute God's justification as gift (or grace) by allowing it to become a human or political achievement.[23]

[22] Miranda, *Marx and The Bible*, p. viii.
[23] Paul is fond of Leviticus 18:5 (cf. Galatians 3:12; Romans 2:13), which emphasizes in its pre-Pauline usage that moral obedience to the Mosaic statutes issues in life. Paul calls this legal justice "righteousness of the law" (Romans 10:5). But when Paul wrests Deuteronomy 30:12f. out of its original Deuteronomic (and prophetic) context and counterposes "what Moses writes" (Romans 10:5) with "what the justice which is of faith says" (Romans 10:6), we stand at the outer boundary of moral, political, and economic interpretation of the gospel. It is only this view of justice *sola fide* that permits, indeed necessitates, gentile inclusion and prevents Paul from being har-

This feature of God's justice makes it impossible to define liberation theology in categories determined by Marxist views of economic justice, whatever brand of Marxism one chooses.

In *Marx Against the Marxists*[24] Miranda denounces the Marxists' distortions of the humanism of the early Marx, their false notions of Marx's economic determinism, glorifications of party power, and wholesale assault on human rights, with a zeal that has only one parallel—Miranda's denunciation of Western Christians who for nineteen centuries have accommodated the justice of God to the violence of the profit system. This rationale seems to leave us with a situation of complete idealism and complete despair regarding both Christianity and Marxism—complete idealism, because what the prophets and the New Testament declare of interhuman justice is perceivable only as an idea, just as in the case of the humanistic Marx; complete despair, because both Marxism and Christianity clearly show how stubbornly imperfectible human beings actually are. Thus the assumption that biblical teaching mandates a single economic ideology for human liberation is, at best, suspect. Correspondingly, the exclusion of gay/lesbian liberation from the genre of liberation theology on the basis of unproven economic presuppositions is the obscuring of one error by another.

This same openness of liberation theology is implicit in "hermeneutical circulation." The meaning of the text is never brought to final completion because someone else's ideological bias has been exposed and corrected. It is my own bias, alas, that must take its own turn in the refiner's fire of criticism, because the freedom we human beings seek is always beyond us, subject to the final disposition of God alone. I wish to show that gay/lesbian liberation can bring new, corrective insights to the interpretations of the sexual majority. At the same time it will profit in its own perceptions of human freedom by entering into the hermeneutical circle. For this

---

monized with James 2:14ff. So Ernst Käsemann, *Commentary on Romans*, trans. and ed. G.W. Bromiley (Grand Rapids, MI: Wm. B. Eerdmans, 1980), pp. 285–87, correctly opposes H.J. Schoeps' use of covenant thought against Paul. Correspondingly, economic ideology, whether communist or capitalist, cannot be the necessary premise of evangelical theology. That would be to reconstitute the circumcision dispute settled in Galatians. On the same ground of faith righteousness, heterosexuality as the necessary prerequisite of Christian freedom is overruled, and homosexual inclusion is created.

[24]José Miranda, *Marx Against the Marxists: The Christian Humanism of Karl Marx*, trans. John Drury (Maryknoll, NY: Orbis Books, 1980).

reason a substantial moral claim can be made for the inclusion of gays/lesbians among the world's poor, alongside the exploited third world, women, blacks and other ethnic deprived, handicapped, elderly, and any others who can lay claim to God's liberative justice.

FACTORS IN MODERN SEXOLOGY CONTRIBUTING TO A NEW HERMENEUTICAL SITUATION

Biblical interpretation can never be divorced from other domains of human reflection and discovery. When the church of the seventeenth century sought to repress Galileo's support of the Copernican view of the solar system because it contradicted scripture, the church had on its hands a hermeneutical revolution. The attempted repression was a diminishment, not an enhancement, of biblical authority.[25] The following considerations cannot, by the nature of the case, claim to be God's final truth, but they possess the potential for helping us, using Brown's words, "to approach the text in a new way," especially if we are prepared to recognize that exegesis without presuppositions is impossible.[26]

[25] In a cogent discussion of "Gayness and Homosexuality: Issues for the Church," in *Embodiment: An Approach to Sexuality and Christian Theology* (Minneapolis: Augsburg, 1978), pp. 180–210), James B. Nelson borrows four interpretative principles from James T. Clemons, "Toward a Christian Affirmation of Human Sexuality," *Religion in Life* 43 (1974):425–35. These are in summary (1) Jesus Christ is the bearer of God's invitation to human wholeness and communion, the central norm by which everything in scripture should be measured; (2) interpretation "must take seriously both the historical context of the biblical writer and our present cultural situation"; (3) biblical study should proceed "with awareness of the cultural relativity in which we ourselves are immersed, and through which we perceive and experience what faith means"; (4) interpretation "should be informed by the revelation of God's truth in other disciplines of human inquiry" (Nelson, *Embodiment*, pp. 181f).

[26] Objective, scientific interpretation of scripture is attacked by Walter Wink, *The Bible in Human Transformation* (Philadelphia: Fortress Press, 1973), p. 1. Working from Descartes' subject/object categories, Wink asserts that "historical biblical criticism is bankrupt." For those who already deplored the rise of the historical method as an abortive compromise of biblical authority, Wink's pronouncement is something less than reassurance, because he sees historical criticism as the necessary emancipation from culturally controlled exegesis. After all, one may add, Paul had to give up his perception of himself as "blameless" before the law (Philippians 3:6) before faith justification appeared to him.

Wink's psychotherapeutic ("human transformation") mode of interpretation, adapted from the work of San Francisco's Dr. Elizabeth Howes, has nuances of liberationist thought, even if it is more subjective-psychological than sociopolitical in its presuppositions.

Structuralism is also seen by some as a revolt against historical criticism. Cf.

Homosexuality is a new word. Words fix meanings. New words can produce new meanings, but not if other, unintended meanings are read into them. The word homosexuality, or homosexual, was not introduced into English (from German) until 1892.[27] The derivation is not from latin *homo* meaning man (in the generic sense) or person, but from Greek *homoios,* meaning like, or same. Thus homosexuality has to do with same-sex orientation, males to males or females to females. Emphasis on orientation rather than on conduct or genital acts is appropriate, because as Alan P. Bell and Martin S. Weinberg point out, homosexuals often enter into heterosexual marriage contracts and conceive children in order to conform to standards set by the heterosexual majority.[28] Furthermore, under conditions of sexual segregation as may occur in prisons,[29] hospitals, and military life, same-sex acts increase in frequency among those whose preference is heterosexual.

The relevance of a correct terminology in treating the topic of homosexuality in biblical literature immediately faces the obvious difficulty that homosexuality is not a biblical word, having been coined only during the latter half of the nineteenth century. An analogy may serve to clarify what is at issue.

The clinical, scientific definition of leprosy (Hansen's disease) was

---

Dan O. Via, *Kerygma and Comedy in the New Testament* (Philadelphia: Fortress Press, 1975), pp. 4–6. But again, structuralism, while emphasizing that meaning is not an endless tracing of cause and effect through time (diachronically) but emerges contemporaneously within patterns of repeated social perceptions (synchronically), is not applied antihistorically by all its advocates.

[27] R.W. Burchfield, ed., *A Supplement to the Oxford English Dictionary,* vol. 2, H–N (Oxford: Clarendon Press, 1976), p. 136. This was in a translation by C.G. Chaddock of the seventh edition of Richard Krafft-Ebing's *Psychopathia Sexualis.* The translation was published by F.A. Davis Co., Philadelphia and London, in 1892. In James Chesebro, ed., *Gayspeak: Gay Male and Lesbian Communication* (New York: Pilgrim Press, 1981), p. 326, n. 8, the coining of homosexual/homosexuality is ascribed to Karoly Maria Benkert (pseudonym Kertbeny) in 1869; but I have been unable to confirm this. John Boswell, *Christianity, Social Tolerance, and Homosexuality* (Chicago: University of Chicago Press, 1980), p. 42, n. 4, found "homosexual instincts" in *A Problem in Modern Ethics* by John Addington Symonds, published in 1891.

[28] Alan P. Bell and Martin S. Weinberg, *Homosexualities: A Study of Diversity Among Men and Women* (New York: Simon & Schuster, 1978), pp. 160f. This is also discussed in William Masters and Virginia Johnson, *Homosexuality in Perspective* (New York: Little, Brown, 1979), pp. 38f., 244.

[29] For a grim account of this, see Carl Weiss and David J. Friar, *Terror in the Prisons* (Indianapolis: Bobbs-Merrill, 1974).

not achieved until 1871, when the microscopic bacteria were isolated and examined by Norwegian physician G.H.A. Hansen. Biblical translators have recognized that the phenomenon called leprosy in scripture cannot, manifestly, conform to the contemporary clinical definition. This fact has led translators of *The New English Bible* to abandon the term leprosy[30] in translating Leviticus 13—14.[30] The 1611 *King James Version* did not use homosexual or homosexuality. A logical argument can thus be made that any discussion of homosexuality in scripture can only multiply confusion because clinical evidence in the relevant passages is not accessible. Modern translations use the word sparingly, if at all.

Another new word is homophobia. The term homophobia, meaning the fear and hatred of homosexuals, was not coined until 1972.[31] The hermeneutical importance of this word can be seen in the light of ideological suspicion. It describes the psychosocial attitudes to which the homosexual must respond, attitudes of pervasive revulsion, condemnation. Insofar as homosexuals internalize the public revulsion as self-hate, they are also homophobic. Gay/lesbian liberation seeks to deal with both these manifestations: (1) the fear/ rejection that exists in the sexual majority and the institutions it controls and (2) the internalization of this fear/rejection in the homosexual community.

Homosexuality is not a pathological condition. The analogy from

---

[30]As to the Hebrew noun for "leprosy" (*tsarʿat,* plus some derivatives with the same stem), Martin Noth (*Leviticus: A Commentary,* rev. ed., ed. and trans. J.E. Anderson, Old Testament Library (Philadelphia: Westminster Press, 1977) uses the word only in quotation marks to alert the reader to the translation problem. He comments (pp. 105f.) on Leviticus 13:2–46: "It is doubtful whether it is here a matter of the real incurable disease of leprosy, for the possibility is envisaged of a disappearance and healing of the signs of illness. The characteristic symptoms of real leprosy at an advanced stage are not mentioned. It is clearly rather a variety of virulent or nonvirulent skin diseases that is being considered here, having cultically 'unclean' effects; but not enough is said about the attendant symptoms for us to be able to define them more precisely." *The New English Bible* translates *tsarʿat* in these passages as "malignant skin disease."

C. Creighton, "Leprosy, Leper," in *Encyclopaedia Biblica,* ed. T.K. Cheyne and J.S. Black (New York: Macmillan, 1902), III:col. 2763, affirms that Greek *lepra* got connected with elephantiasis graecorum (Hansen's disease) in medieval medical writings and was confused after that. These comments show that modern medical understanding cannot content itself with unexamined popular meanings but requires its own form of ideological suspicion.

[31]George Weinberg, *Society and the Healthy Homosexual* (New York: St. Martin's Press, 1972), pp. 1–21.

biblical words for leprosy would be misleading if one mistakenly concluded from it that homosexuality (like Hansen's disease) is a state of medical pathology.

On December 15, 1973, the trustees of the American Psychiatric Association (APA) removed homosexuality from its official nomenclature of mental disorders. Simultaneously, the APA trustees deplored "all public and private discrimination against homosexuals in such areas as employment, housing, public accommodations, and licensing." The same action was taken by the American Psychological Association on January 24, 1975.

Removing homosexuality from the section on sexual deviation in the *Diagnostic and Statistical Manual,* where it stood along with fetishism, voyeurism, pedophilia, and exhibitionism, the APA put in its place "sexual orientation disturbance," further defined as follows:

> This category is for individuals whose sexual interests are primarily directed towards people of the same sex and who are either disturbed by, in conflict with, or wish to change their sexual orientation. This diagnostic category is distinguished from homosexuality which, by itself, does not necessarily constitute a psychiatric disorder.[32]

In June of 1973 Robert L. Spitzer, a member of the APA task force on Nomenclature and Statistics, composed a rationale for the change reflected in the above quotation. Dr. Spitzer explained:

> For a mental or psychiatric condition to be considered a psychiatric disorder, it must either regularly cause subjective distress or regularly be associated with some general impairment in social effectiveness or functioning.[33]

Because many homosexuals experience no significant "subjective distress" regarding their sexual orientation, despite the power of the homophobic environment, and function effectively in their vocations, negative prejudgment about homosexual pathology is medically and morally inappropriate.

Modern sex research documents the relativity of sexual orientation. In 1938 some female students at Indiana University requested that a course on marriage be offered. Alfred Kinsey, a biologist, became part of this effort. Ten years later, under auspices of the

---

[32] Press release of the American Psychiatric Association, 1700 18th St., NW, Washington, DC 20009, December 15, 1973.

[33] Robert L. Spitzer, "A Proposal About Homosexuality and the APA Nomenclature: Homosexuality as One Form of Sexual Behavior and Sexual Orientation Disturbance as a Psychiatric Disorder," June 7, 1973. This rationale paper was attached to the APA press release mentioned in n. 32.

Institute for Sex Research, appeared his massive study on *Sexual Behavior in the Human Male*, followed five years later by *Sexual Behavior in the Human Female.*[34] Freud had already written of *absolute* inverts (those of exclusively same-sex orientation), *amphigenic* inverts (those equally attracted to the same or other sex), and *contingent* inverts (those persuaded under certain conditions to undertake same-sex activity).[35] The Kinsey publications further relativized the meanings of homosexual and heterosexual, telling of "endless gradations" in a scale from zero (exclusive heterosexuality) to six (exclusive homosexuality), concluding that "it is impossible to determine the number of persons who are 'homosexual' or 'heterosexual.' It is only possible to determine how many persons belong, at any particular time, to each of the classifications on a heterosexual-homosexual scale."[36]

Based on an unprecedented volume of case studies, Kinsey reported that 37 percent of the male population had at least some overt homosexual experience to the point of orgasm between adolescence and old age, that is, two males out of every five. One male in thirteen (8 percent) was exclusively homosexual for at least three years between ages sixteen and sixty-five, although Kinsey found only 4 percent of the white males to be exclusively homosexual throughout their lives after adolescence.[37] For those primarily or exclusively homosexual, Kinsey found female responses and behavior approximately one-third to one-half as prevalent as that of males.[38] In 1974, continuing the work of the Kinsey Institute, Martin Weinberg and Colin Williams reinforced the bisexual or ambisexual emphasis, reiterating that "eighteen per cent of the males have at least as much of the homosexual as the heterosexual in their histories for at least three years between the age of sixteen and seventy-five. This is more than one in six of the white male population."[39]

The facts of bisexuality, the frequency of same-sex behavior, and

---

[34]Alfred C. Kinsey, W.B. Pomeroy, and C.E. Martin, *Sexual Behavior in the Human Male* (Philadelphia: W.B. Saunders, 1948; Alfred C. Kinsey, W.B. Pomeroy, C.E. Martin, and P.H. Gebhard, *Sexual Behavior in the Human Female* (Philadelphia: W.B. Saunders, 1953).

[35]Sigmund Freud, *Three Essays on the Theory of Sexuality*, trans. and ed. James Strachey (London: Hogarth, 1974), pp. 2–3.

[36]Kinsey, *Human Male*, p. 650; *Human Female*, p. 472.

[37]Kinsey, *Human Male*, pp. 650f.

[38]Kinsey, *Human Female*, p. 475.

[39]Martin S. Weinberg and Colin J. Williams, *Male Homosexuals: Their Problems and Adaptations* (New York: Oxford University Press, 1974), p. 207.

evidence for a sliding scale of sexual orientation affected by age and circumstance require still further modifications in the sexual consciousness one brings to ancient biblical texts, even if it is conceded that moral norms are not totally determined by statistical information on sexual behavior.

Sex therapists emphasize identical patterns of sexual responsiveness. William Masters and Virginia Johnson have reinforced conclusions of the Kinsey school on the basis of treatment of dysfunction and dissatisfaction (i.e., the desire to convert or revert to heterosexuality) in the sex life of male and female homosexuals in the years 1968 through 1977 and have published their findings.[40] Their contributions to sexual knowledge are pertinent in significant ways to the exposition of biblical texts.

Masters and Johnson repeatedly affirm (e.g., pp. 122, 124, 203, 205f., 226) that the heterosexual boast "my way is better than your way," when measuring functional efficiency in response to sexual stimulation, is groundless. They apply a wide array of stimulative techniques in treating sexual dysfunction in both hetero- and homosexual clients, with identical results in both groups. Supported by extensive clinical verification, this discovery applies to the physiological trajectory of arousal, orgasm, and postorgasmic resolution charted by these therapists (pp. 126f.). Although some would contend that the identity of physiological responsiveness in the homo- and heterosexual groups does not affect the moral judgment to be rendered in either case, it would be affected in instances in which the judgment proved itself influenced by mistaken assumptions regarding physiological factors involved in sexual interchange. As a result, Masters and Johnson can therefore with reason speculate that "when absorbed, this finding should lead to significant modification in current cultural concepts."[41]

Not only do they concur in and make use of the Kinsey sex preference scale, but they also constitute a specific ambisexual group made up of Kinsey three (middle of the spectrum) subjects. By *ambisexual* they mean a man or woman "who unreservedly enjoys, solicits, or responds to overt sexual opportunity with equal ease and interest regardless of the sex of the partners, and who, as a sexually mature individual, has never evidenced interest in a con-

[40] William Masters and Virginia Johnson, *Homosexuality in Perspective* (Boston: Little, Brown, 1979).
[41] Ibid., p. 226.

tinuing relationship."[42] The reference to continuing relationship is rather striking and evokes moral reflection.

Although the two therapists disavow any invasion of moral and theological judgment on the subject of homosexuality[43]—their scientific commitment precludes, presumably, any such invasion— the definition of ambisexual that they adopt involves a "constant partner rotation" that can invite sexual boredom and surrender of desired psychosocial partner interchange.[44] This in turn might well eventuate in an intolerable "aloneness," especially in advanced years. Implicit in these observations is a bent toward committed relationship, even if that relationship is valued on the basis of a pragmatic philosophy consisting of functional/dysfunctional criteria in sexual performance.

Widely diverse homosexual life-styles often defy the reputation of profligacy popularly ascribed to the gay/lesbian world. By the title chosen for their work—*Homosexualities: A Study of Diversity Among Men and Women*—Bell and Weinberg emphasize that the social behavior and attitudes of homosexuals do not, any more than for heterosexuals, lend themselves to a simplistic reductionism modeled after the "orgy room" at a gay bath.

In an interviewing process conducted in 1969–70, 979 white and black, male and female homosexuals and 477 white and black, male and female heterosexuals of the San Francisco Bay area were questioned carefully for the descriptive data finally yielding their five behavioral categories. By "close-coupled" the authors refer to partners who are "closely bound together" and who "tend to look to each other rather than outsiders for sexual and interpersonal satisfactions."[45] Such partners spend more evenings at home, seldom frequent bars or baths. Their sexual lives seem to gratify them. Police encounters are minimal; trouble at work, assault and robbery experiences, infrequent. Both males and females were more contented and self-accepting, less despondent and lonely than those in the other four groups described below. The evidence encourages further analogies among the close-coupled to well-married heterosexuals.

Among the "open-coupled," Bell and Weinberg's second group-

---

[42] Ibid., pp. 154f.
[43] Ibid., p. 403.
[44] Ibid., pp. 222–23.
[45] Bell and Weinberg, *Homosexualities*, p. 214.

ing, cruising was above average among males and females. More sexual activity and broader sexual repertoires were also found, but partners had less success at meeting or fulfilling sexual requests on one another. In happiness, exuberance, depression, tenseness, paranoia, worry, and other features of social adjustment, the open-coupled were not distinguishable from the average homosexual respondent,[46] although lesbians were lower in self-acceptance than homosexual males and evidenced more apparent difficulty with the open-coupled arrangement than did the men.

"Functionals" were like "swinging singles" among heterosexuals: more sexual activity; among females, more marriages; minimal regret over being homosexual; frequent cruising; much involvement in gay/lesbian culture. The most exuberant and overt, these were "the most likely ever to have been arrested, booked or convicted for a 'homosexual' offense."[47] By comparison with the close-coupled, the functionals, despite their optimism and being at ease with their sexuality, did not meet the level of adjustment to homosexual orientation evidenced by the former.

The fourth class, called "dysfunctionals," most clearly conformed to the stereotype of the tormented homosexual.[48] They were troubled, regretful, prone to worry about their sexual preference. Males experienced worry over sexual performance: impotence, premature ejaculation. Lesbians felt need for extended counseling for emotional problems. One male complained of others' shallowness, their indifference to lasting relationships, "and yet he's had more than a thousand partners in the past two years."[49]

The "asexuals" were the lowest in frequency of sexual activity. Lonely and unhappy, they had trouble finding a partner but were less interested in sex anyway. They rated their sex appeal very low, had "narrow sexual repertoires." Asexual lesbians showed proneness to seek professional help for their sexual orientation but gave up the treatment quickly. Alongside the dysfunctionals, asexuals differed in their "disengagement from others, . . . lack of involvement with friends," and indifference to the range and depth of human experience.

Bell and Weinberg conclude from their taxonomy of homosexual

[46] Ibid., p. 222.
[47] Ibid., pp. 224f.
[48] Ibid., p. 225.
[49] Ibid., p. 226.

behavior that relatively few homosexuals conform to the stereotype of irresponsible degeneracy.

Investigation of the causes (etiology) of homosexuality makes doubtful, if not completely unbelievable, a considerable amount of classic psychoanalytic theory. From the same fifteen hundred or so homosexual and heterosexual subjects interviewed in the San Francisco area in 1969–70 and profiled in Bell and Weinberg's *Homosexualities,* there emerged also the two-volume study of *Sexual Preference: Its Development in Men and Women.*[50] If the result of the former work is to disqualify the assumption that homosexual behavior can be credibly categorized according to a narrow set of popular stereotypes, the result of *Sexual Preference* is to cast doubt on cherished professional theories about the causes of homosexuality, especially those pointing to adverse family circumstances.

One Freudian theory on the cause of male homosexuality emphasizes the impact of matching a passive, detached father and a dominant, possessive mother. In the oedipal struggle against sexual attraction for the mother, the male child overreacts to her seductiveness and overprotection by a general rejection of female sex orientation. This theme played an important part in the 1967 CBS television report called "The Homosexuals." Using "path analysis" (p. 21),[51] which emerged from biological sciences as a way of testing data from a large number of independent variables as to their validation of a complex developmental process (or "path") required by a given theory, the researchers concluded that maternal-trait variables showing differences between homosexual and heterosexual respondents "were found to have almost no effect on adult sex orientation" (p. 47). Despite much psychoanalytic opinion to the contrary, the data compiled in *Sexual Preference* "seem flatly to contradict the notion that during childhood homosexual males identify with their mothers more than do heterosexual males" (p. 50).

The "cold father" is said to impede the acquiring of a firm sense of masculinity essential to heterosexual preference in the male offspring (p. 59). The evidence reported does show more difference in the attitude of homosexuals toward their fathers than toward their

[50]Alan P. Bell, Martin S. Weinberg, and Sue K. Hammersmith, *Sexual Preference: Its Development in Men and Women,* 2 vols. (Bloomington: Indiana University Press, 1981).
[51]Page references are to volume 1 of this work, which is an interpretation of the data contained in volume 2.

mothers; but the relatively negative appraisal of these fathers "has little eventual influence" (p. 62) on the sexual preference of male homosexuals.

The mother-dominated father turns out to be the weakest of the fifteen variables measured for the prediction of homosexual propensity, so the Kinsey Institute researchers conclude that "it does not appear from our data that the way their parents got along with each other had much to do with respondents' sex preference in adulthood" (p. 66).

Sexual Preference, chapter 7, on gender conformity, discloses that prehomosexual boys are, in their perceptions of themselves, more removed from stereotypically "boy" activity (football, scouts, etc.). This in turn relates to homosexual arousal before age nineteen, a perceived gender-related difference from other boys, delayed sex interest in girls, and adult same-sex preference. Bell, Weinberg, and Hammersmith conclude, nevertheless, using path analysis for assessing the causal connections between the interrelated elements, that result rather than cause is the more likely of the two alternative explanations.

The classic (Freudian) theory of penis envy in the development of female sexuality fares no better than other time-honored hypotheses. The female child is said to devalue the mother because she has not supplied the child with a penis. Erotic rivalry with the mother for the father's affection further intensifies maternal conflict through fear of abandonment by the mother. A warm mother-daughter relationship, however, encourages the child to repress erotic attachment to the father, to seek a more eligible male, and thus to acquire a vicarious penis leading to maternal fulfillment, preferably in the birth of a son (p. 98). A negative application of this view supposes that unloving mother-daughter relationships impel the child toward substitute mothers in the form of female lovers. Poor relations with mothers have been frequently cited in the etiology of lesbianism (p. 118). Testing the causative force of harsh, unpleasant mother relationships, however, yielded almost no positive results, and the "hostile, rejecting mother" proved itself to be fourteenth in rank of potency among the fifteen variables used as predictors of lesbian preference (p. 120).

While holding that a considerable volume of modern research indicates a biological basis for some instances of homosexuality (p. 220), these writers do not feel this is inconsistent with their own findings should it be fully confirmed. Their work seems to presuppose the Kinsey philosophy (followed also by Masters and Johnson) that homosexuality is a learned phenomenon, people beginning at birth with an undirected sexual potential. If organic or body-chemical explanations should, however, prevail, we are reminded (pp. 218f.) how this would make even more indefensible moral condemnation of same-sex preference or assertions of its unnaturalness.

In summary, contemporary biblical interpretation faces a tremendous challenge in the widening influence of liberation theology. It is increasingly evident that historical exegesis, discovering objectively the meaning of the text in its own time, may only render us blind and deaf to the present meaning mediated by sources of enlightenment not yet taken seriously. Liberation theology itself is challenged by the gay/lesbian movement to embrace excluded millions whose experience of oppression and cry for justice are no less real because official church councils have not yet incorporated their outcry in the urgent agenda of social ministry. Too long already have we in the religious community waited for the bondage of homophobic thinking to be challenged at its base: tradition-bound biblical ideas. We move forward now to the specific elements of this challenge.

CHAPTER/TWO

Sodom Revisited:
An Inquiry into the History of
Morals

Perhaps nowhere in the history of morals has biblical literature played a more explicit, although negative, role than in the case of the Sodom narrative in Genesis 19:1–29. Although we are occasionally reminded that this tale also recounts the deliverance of Lot, an example of divine condescension and mercy, references to Sodom in writing and speaking, in law and religion, are, nonetheless, grim reminders of unredeemable degradation matched by a divine, relentless retribution. "Sodomy" is a code word that encapsulates the moral heritage of those fierce verses that have branded on human remembrance across the centuries the fire and brimstone rained by God on the disobedient, without respect to age or gender. Although speaking more broadly than with reference to homosexuality alone, Alfred Kinsey writes:

> There is nothing in the English-American social structure which has had more influence upon present patterns of sexual behavior than the religious grounds of that culture. It would require long research and a complete volume to work out the origins of the present-day religious codes which apply to sex, of the present-day sex mores, of the coded sex laws, and to trace the subtle ways in which these have influenced the behavior of individuals. . . . Our particular systems certainly go back to the Old Testament philosophy on which the Talmud is based, and which was the philosophy of those Jews who first followed the Christian faith.[1]

[1] Alfred C. Kinsey, W.B. Pomeroy, and C.E. Martin, *Sexual Behavior in the Human Male* (Philadelphia: W.B. Saunders, 1948), p. 465.

In his tracing of the legal antecedents that underlay the severe medieval proscriptions of homosexual acts and that carried over into the modern period, D.S. Bailey found the sixth-century legal reforms of Christian emperor Justinian centrally significant. The logic of Justinian rested unmistakably on Genesis 19, according to conventional understanding of the passage. Justinian's 77th Novella, promulgated in A.D. 538, asserted:

> Since certain men, seized by diabolical incitement, practise among themselves the most disgraceful lusts, and act contrary to nature: we enjoin them to take to heart the fear of God and the judgment to come, and to abstain from suchlike diabolical and unlawful lusts, so that they may not be visited by the just wrath of God on account of these impious acts, with the result that cities perish with all their inhabitants. For we are taught by the Holy Scriptures that because of like impious conduct cities have indeed perished, together with the men in them.[2]

This chapter reexamines Sodom and sodomy with the conscious reservation that there is no valid way to determine whether any of "the men of Sodom, both young and old, all the people to the last man [Gen. 19:4]," who surrounded Lot's house and were apparently prepared to engage in homosexual rape, were homosexuals. Lot has prospective sons-in-law (Genesis 19:12–14). The logical inference must be that every last man in Sodom would not have been homosexual, regardless of the emphatic language of Genesis 19:4, and that what we are dealing with in this case is an episode of gang rape.

Another preliminary consideration arising from sociological criticism of the text is that the narrative is totally patriarchal in focus. The women of Sodom remain as faceless as they are nameless. Are they also part of the rape-bent gang, and can they and their children together with all the men and boys be justly subjected to an indiscriminate doom that would inspire Justinian, centuries later, to

[2]D.S. Bailey, *Homosexuality and the Western Christian Tradition* (London: Longmans, Green, 1955), p. 73. John Boswell, *Christianity, Social Tolerance, and Homosexuality* (Chicago: University of Chicago Press, 1980), pp. 172f., criticizes Bailey for ignoring the fact that Justinian's *motive* in making same-sex acts a capital offense was not really to turn Christian moral principles into civil law, because Novella 140 permits, on the basis of common consent, the dissolution of a marriage contract, contrary to the New Testament and the church fathers. Boswell supports Edward Gibbon's position (*The Decline and Fall of the Roman Empire*, ed. O. Smeaton, vol. 4 ([New York: E.P. Dutton, 1910], p. 439) that the law on homosexual acts (Gibbon uses paederasty) was a guise for charging those "to whom no crime could be imputed."

canonize the fire and brimstone by requiring the death penalty for homosexual behavior? And what moral precept is to be derived from Lot's offering of his two virgin daughters to appease the lustful mob about to storm the door (Genesis 19:8)? If it is urged that contemporary notions of women's rights cannot with equity be used to denigrate the social conduct of ancient men, we are all the more obliged to discover why only selected features of a tradition attain moral normativeness, indeed those very features that reinforce the power of the strong and increase the vulnerability of the disempowered.

The fact of the case is that nothing of lesbian acts is mentioned in all of Old Testament literature. They are found in the New Testament only at Romans 1:26, a passage whose purpose in the rhetorical scheme of that letter may be quite otherwise than conventionally proposed.

It is a redundancy to speak of the androcentricity of the patriarchal narratives, but the link between homosexuality, homophobia, and patriarchy commands more serious reflection. In his denunciation of same-sex practices Chrysostom thunders: "What shall we say of this insanity, which is worse than fornication? For I maintain that not only are you made by it into a woman, but you also cease to be a man."[3] In the ancient Middle East the practice of subjecting the defeated enemy to anal penetration has been clearly established.[4] Kenneth Dover reminds us "that human societies at many times and in many regions have subjected strangers, newcomers and trespassers to homosexual anal violation as a way of reminding them of their subordinate status."[5] Was this, within the ethos of patriarchy, the ultimate emasculation: reduction to womanhood? In his classic on Greek education Henrì-Irénée Marrou describes the extensive role played by the erotic attachment of young boys to adult male lovers, an attachment known among the Greeks as *paiderastia*, but not with the psychopathological or morally delinquent connotations of the English *pederasty*. Greek pederastic education served a deep male

[3] St. John Chrysostom's *Commentary on Romans*, Homily 4, cited from Boswell, *Christianity, Social Tolerance, and Homosexuality*, p. 361.

[4] Cf. Peter Coleman, *Christian Attitudes to Homosexuality* (London: SPCK, 1980), pp. 34, 54. In the mythological account of Horus' nocturnal subjection to the female role by Seth, although the act is intercrural (i.e., "between the thighs"), Horus suffers scorn, while Seth is rewarded. See William K. Simpson, *The Literature of Ancient Egypt*, new ed. (New Haven, CT: Yale University Press, 1973), pp. 20–21.

[5] Kenneth J. Dover, *Greek Homosexuality* (Cambridge, MA: Harvard University Press, 1978), p. 105.

need to realize manhood itself and is thus called by Marrou "a misogynous ideal of total masculinity."[6] Although aspects of the connection between male dominance and homosexuality or homophobia must await further empirical illumination, it is already widely acknowledged that the sociological assumptions of patriarchal traditions are manifestly inadequate for the formation of a modern Judeo-Christian ethic of heterosexual relations, whether genital or otherwise. This should also alert us to the danger of moral deductions about homoeroticism based on those same texts, especially if these deductions are shut off from sexological insights arising from the kind of scientific inquiry narrated in Chapter One.

In the following examination of Hermann Gunkel's and Sherwin Bailey's expositions of Genesis 19, my intent is to show that Gunkel, although a pioneer of historical exegesis, was limited by nineteenth-century presuppositions about homosexuality and thus served to perpetuate homophobic oppression. Bailey's interpretation, however, was based on a valid liberationist commitment but can be faulted on historical exegetical grounds. Both writers contribute in their own ways, however, to a new liberationist understanding of Genesis 19 serving that kind of theology proposed by James Cone when he declared it to be "a rational study of the being of God in the world in the light of the existential situation of an oppressed community, relating the forces of liberation to the essence of the gospel, which is Jesus Christ."[7]

HERMANN GUNKEL ON GENESIS 19

At Genesis 19:1 Lot receives two angel visitors (a significant number), urgently persuades them not to spend the night on the street, brings them to his house, and feasts them in accord with the protocol of hospitality already graciously observed by Abraham at the oaks of Mamre in 18:1ff. Lot does not know who these emissaries are, nor that the holocaust of judgment is about to consume the city, despite the pleas of Abraham (18:22–33). With masterful brevity the narrator confirms the foreboding that already hangs over the peaceful scene as sated guests prepare for a comfortable night's rest. The

[6]Henrì-Irénée Marrou, *Histoire de l'education dans l'antiquite,* 6th ed. (Paris: Editions de Seuil, 1965), p. 44.
[7]James Cone, *A Black Theology of Liberation* (Philadelphia: J.B. Lippincott, 1970), p. 17.

house is suddenly surrounded by the whole male population of the city, "both young and old."[8] Ominously, the men and boys of Sodom call out to Lot, "Where are the men who came to you tonight? Bring them out to us, that we might know them [Gen. 19:5]." Gunkel finds in the intended attack on Lot's guests pederastic rape! He comments:

> The ancient saga views the crime of child rape (Knabenschändung) as something completely atrocious: such a city has earned fire and brimstone! Israel conceives unnatural lewdness of that sort as "abomination" (Lev. 18:22) and as specifically Canaanite (Lev. 20:13, 23). The "men" are represented as youths in the bloom of life whose fresh beauty excites the evil lust of the Sodomites. This supposition is significant from the history-of-religions standpoint: so in earliest times did they conceive of many deities. At the time of the narrator, angels were so conceived, cf. also Tobit 5:4ff., Mark 16:5, and later the transfigured deceased (Apocalypse of Peter, 4–16).
>
> In ancient Israel Jahwe scarcely turns out as a fresh and blooming youth, but is represented as a mature man, as mighty warrior. These considerations also show that the primary meaning of the story has hardly been that Jahwe was among the "men." The idea that the Sodomites would have attempted child rape on Jahwe would be too crass even for the earliest Hebrew saga.[9]

It is doubtful that any modern reader with only an English translation at hand would ever picture the scene at Genesis 19:5 as an illustration of attempted pederastic rape; nor can it be supported by appeal to the Hebrew behind the English. Ideological suspicion readily suggests that Gunkel has introduced pederastic assault from a cultural milieu in which homosexuality was conceived entirely from the standpoint of Greek *paiderastia*, the sexual love of an adult male for a boy, not in the morally affirmative, educationally

---

[8] Gerhard von Rad, *Genesis: A Commentary*, 3d Eng. ed., trans. John H. Marks, Old Testament Library (Philadelphia: Westminster Press, 1972), p. 212. The age of "young" (Hebrew *na^{c}ar*) is wholly unspecified. The word refers to an infant, for example, at Exodus 2:6; 1 Samuel 1:24; 4:21.

[9] Hermann Gunkel, *Genesis*, 3. Aufl., Göttinger Handkommentar zum Alten Testament (Göttingen: Vandenhoeck & Ruprecht, 1910), p. 208. I have interpreted the abbreviation "Mak" in Gunkel as "Mark" and "Ap. Pt." as the Akhmin text of the Apocalypse of Peter in M. R. James, *The Apocryphal New Testament* (Oxford: Clarendon Press, 1953), pp. 507–10. The Greek text of the latter consulted in this connection was not that of Bouriant cited by Gunkel but of E. Klostermann, *Kleine Texte fuer theologische Vorlesungen und Uebungen*, Nr. 3 (Bonn: A. Marcus und E. Weber, 1908), p. 9.

beneficial sense of the Greeks,[10] but in the morally degenerate sense written into civil law at the time of Justinian.

Although *homosexual* had entered the German vocabulary in the writings of Krafft-Ebing (cf. Chapter One, n. 27) by the last decade of the nineteenth century, classical education (in preparation for theological study) continued to refer to same-sex behavior as *Knabenliebe* ("boy love"), which literally renders the Greek *paiderastia,* or pederasty. For example, the distinguished Pauly-Wissowa encyclopedia of classical antiquity[11] has no entry under the noun *Homosexualität* but only the article on *Knabenliebe* by Wilhelm Kroll in Volume 21.[12] From *Knabenliebe* to *Knabenschändung* (Gunkel's word for discussion of Genesis 19:5ff.) is a short semantic step within homophobic culture.[13] This can also be demonstrated from the famous Grimm dictionary of 1873, which was closer to the time of Gunkel's education than to the present. It has no entry under *Homosexualität* and explains *Knabenliebe* as a translation of Greek *paiderastia* in the manner already indicated from Pauly-Wissowa. It proceeds, however, going much further than Pauly-Wissowa, to equate *Knabenliebe* with *Knabenschänderai* (or *Knabenschändung,* sexual molestation of a male child by an adult

[10] Discussing homosexuality in his introduction to Plato's *Symposium,* K.J. Dover, ed., *Symposium,* by Plato (London: Cambridge University Press, 1980), pp. 4f., writes: "Any relationship between an older and a younger male in a Greek community had an educational dimension which was necessarily lacking in a relationship between a man and a woman, since the younger, destined to become an adult male, could take the older as a model to be imitated, and this stimulated the older to become, and remain, worth imitating. That is why the homosexual response of a man to the visual stimulus afforded by a handsome boy or youth seemed to Plato a good foundation upon which first a teacher-pupil relationship, and then a cooperative intellectual enterprise, could be built."

[11] *Paulys Realencyclopaedia der classischen Altertumswissenschaft,* hrsg. v. Georg Wissowa und Wilhelm Kroll, 73 Bde. (Stuttgart: J.B. Metzler, 1921–68).

[12] Pauly-Wissowa does have additional references to *Knabenliebe,* e.g., under *Kinaidos, Weib,* but the promised article on *Tribades* mentioned at the end of the *Knabenliebe* article by Kroll seems not to have appeared.

[13] Heinz Heger, *The Men with the Pink Triangle,* trans. David Fernbach (Boston: Alyson Publications, 1980), p. 14, affirms that under the twelve years of National Socialism in Germany there were 90,000 civil convictions of homosexuals. How many died in the concentration camps cannot be definitely verified, but Heger holds it "must have been several tens of thousands." Gunkel cannot be blamed, of course, for Nazi oppression of homosexuals; but it is fair to ask how much he was affected by and contributed to the homophobic culture. There must be some exceptions, but Christian resistance to the final solution of the homosexual problem under Nazism appears to have been even less evident than resistance to the "final solution to the Jewish problem."

male).[14] Two additional considerations encourage the conclusion that Gunkel's discovery of pretty boys in the angel guests and attempted pederastic rape of them by the wicked Sodomites is born from cultural conditioning extraneous to the exegesis of Genesis 19.

The first pertains to the texts cited for demonstration of the young age and beauty of the two guests. In the case of Tobit 5:4ff. and Mark 16:5 (cf., p. 28), his appeal is to the Greek noun *neaniskos*, describing an angel as a "young man." The Tobit example is not convincing in that *neaniskos*, although present at verses 5 and 7 in the Sinaiticus manuscript, is lacking in both Alexandrinus and Vaticanus; so the omission of "young man" as attested in the *Authorized Version (King James Version)* may well be correct. The Latin does have the noun *juvenis* ("young man"), but because Charlton Lewis and Charles Short describe such a person as between twenty and forty years of age,[15] the young age implied by "boy" seems inappropriate to the angel of Tobit 5 cited in Gunkel's example. Further, the context discloses nothing of the beauty of Tobit's angel (Raphael).

The aspect of beauty is also lacking for Mark's "young man." The earliest interpreters of Mark, that is, Matthew and Luke, forsake "young man" *(neaniskos)* in Mark 16:5 entirely and revert to "angel" (Matthew 28:2, 5), which is as ageless as the Hebrew *malꞌakim* (angels) in Genesis 19:1. The parallel expression in Luke 24:4 is merely "two men" *(andres duo)*. The passage from the Apocalypse of Peter does describe the beautiful countenance and curly, flowering hair of the transfigured deceased. They are defined, however, not as boys but, again, as "two men" *(duo andres, vs. 6)*. One can add to this that the transfigured deceased in Mark 9:2–8 are not depicted as boys.

Another objection to Gunkel's discovery of pretty boys arises from his handling, following Wellhausen, of Abraham's plea for Sodom in Genesis 18:22–33. He treats these verses as a later supplement, for reasons that can be consigned to a footnote.[16] What-

---

[14] Jacob Grimm und Wilhelm Grimm, Hrsg., *Deutsches Wörterbuch*, Bd. 5 (Leipzig: S. Hirzel, 1873), col. 1325.

[15] Charlton T. Lewis and Charles Short, *A Latin Dictionary* (Oxford: Clarendon Press, 1966), pp. 203–5.

[16] Gunkel, *Genesis*, pp. 203–5. The reasons are as follows. According to Genesis 18:22, "the men" departed from Abraham, but in verse 22 Abraham is still standing before the Lord, who has previously been part of the company of the three men. In 18:20f. the Lord intends to visit Sodom and Gomorrah to investigate the outcry

ever value one may ascribe to the Wellhausen-Gunkel judgment that 18:22-33 is a secondary intrustion into the original sequence, some explanation seems required for the fact that we have three men in 18:2, then two angels in 19:1, followed by a return in 19:17 (Hebrew text) to "he," the Lord, once again united with the angels. The effect of deleting 18:22–33 as a secondary intrusion into the original sequence, means that "the men" of 18:22, that is, the "three men" of 18:2, must carry over into 19:1; and Gunkel insists that this is so,[17] with the exception that the number must become two so as to avoid the gross suggestion that pederastic assault is now attempted on Jahweh as one of "the men." The net result, however, of Gunkel's careful effort to restore "men" as subject in 19:1 renders more remote than ever the notion of beautiful boys as the object of pederastic arousal among the male Sodomites. That von Rad's *Genesis*[18] should still find blooming, youthful beauty in the angel visitors at Sodom and perpetuate the pederastic rape theme illustrates the persisting influence of the Gunkel exegetical heritage as well as the sequacious habits of commentators.

Gunkel's emphasis on the history-of-religions approach provided a basis from which a liberationist interpretation could emerge. By a studied differentiation of saga and history[19] he concluded that Genesis is not history but a collection of sagas, poetic narration of a popular, national sort, handed down through ancient tradition, inculcating religious and social ideas esteemed by various transmitters of the material. Proceeding to establish Genesis 19 in the general world of folklore out of which it emerged, and by appeal to the legend of Philemon and Baucis from Ovid's *Metamorphoses* and

---

against it. In verses 22–33, however, this intention is abandoned. The possibility of delivering Sodom and Gomorrah, furthermore, is not consonant with the resolve already disclosed in 18:17 to destroy the two cities. In the inserted piece Abraham recognizes the deity; but this does not conform to the nonrecognition of 18:1–16. The idea of God as "Judge of all the earth [18:25]" before whom Abraham is as dust and ashes (vs. 27) conflicts with the humanlike deity enjoying bread and meat as Abraham's guest in the first paragraph of chapter 18. Finally, Gunkel discovers in Abraham's intercessory plea a level of unselfish and ecumenical compassion that can have appeared only at a later prophetic period of religious history. Likewise, the possibility of delivering individual righteous ones from a holocaust to be visited on the city as a whole marks a period of individualization exemplified in texts like Deuteronomy 24:16, Ezekiel 18:2ff., and Jeremiah 31:29ff., passages much later in theological outlook than the primary Jahwist stratum of the story.

[17] Ibid., pp. 206–8.
[18] Von Rad, *Genesis*, p. 217.
[19] Gunkel, *Genesis*, pp. VII–XIII.

31

kindred tales,[20] Gunkel shifts the fulcrum of the Sodom episode toward the ethic of hospitality. This theme comes forward in the history of interpretation under liberationist sponsorship, joins issue with the ideology of pederasty on the negative side of the Gunkel legacy, and seeks to drive it from the field.

AN ANTITHETICAL VIEW FROM D. SHERWIN BAILEY

If Gunkel provides a singular example of homophobic stereotypes in his exegesis of Genesis 19, Sherwin Bailey provides an opinion at the opposite arc of the pendulum in his 1955 book, *Homosexuality and the Western Christian Tradition.* Bailey takes up the suggestion by George Barton in the Hastings Encyclopedia[21] that there is no need to understand the verb know in the coital sense when the aggressive Sodomites call out to Lot, "Where are the men who came to you tonight? Bring them out to us, that we may know them." Barton proposes that the meaning may signify nothing more than "get acquainted with."

Baily and Barton are followed in this view by John McNeill[22] and John Boswell.[23] These writers correctly emphasize the moral duty of hospitality accented by Gunkel from parallels in literature of the ancient world and dominant in Genesis 18:1–8. Boswell cites from Homer's *Odyssey* the sobriquet *Zeus xenios,* which underlines the deity's hospitality as protector of guests. Bailey appeals to the fact that 943 uses of the Hebrew verb *yadha^c* ("know") in the Old Testament show the noncoital meaning, whereas there are only ten instances—exclusive of Genesis 19:5 and the parallel to it in Judges 19:22—in which the coital meaning occurs.[24]

If, then, originally the verb know merely signified "get acquainted," how did the coital sense impose itself on Genesis 19:5? Bailey argues that this change intruded at the time of the intertestamental books, Jubilees, 2 Enoch, and the Testament of Naphtali.[25] Following the guidelines of R.H. Charles in his analysis of the com-

---

[20] Ibid., pp. 214–16.

[21] George A. Barton, "Sodomy," *Encyclopaedia of Religion and Ethics,* ed. James Hastings (New York: Charles Scribner's Sons, 1921), 11: 672a; Bailey, *Homosexuality,* p. 3.

[22] John J. McNeill, *The Church and the Homosexual* (Kansas City: Sheed Andrews and McMeel, 1976), pp. 43f.

[23] Boswell, *Christianity, Social Tolerance, and Homosexuality,* pp. 94–97.

[24] Bailey, *Homosexuality,* p. 2, n. 2; the ten occurrences are Genesis 4:1, 17, 25; 19:8; 24:16; 38:26; Judges 11:39; 19:25; 1 Samuel 1:19; 1 Kings 1:4.

[25] Ibid., pp. 9–28.

position and chronology of these books, Bailey fixes a second-century B.C. date (Jubilees) for the first appearance of the sex motif in the history of interpretation. This was not a same-sex violation but a violation of the "orders of being" reflected in the myth of Genesis 6:1–6 and Jude 6–7, in which angels ("watchers" in Jewish tradition) copulated with the daughters of human beings. Finally, at a stratum of Naphtali attributable to the period 70 to 40 B.C., the sin of Sodom is interpreted as same-sex intercourse. Primary evidence for Bailey's argument comes out of 2 Enoch 34:2, Naphtali 3:4f. and 4:1.

Thus it was during the Maccabean period, when conflict with Greek culture—and particularly its tradition of pederasty—was at an acute level, that the sin of Sodom was construed as pederasty or homosexual acts. Philo, Josephus, and the Rabbis adopt the new interpretation. It is found in the Septuagint translation of Genesis 19:5 (*sunginesthai,* "to know sexually") and was taken over in early Christian literature from Jewish antecedents. We have already seen the persistence of this view into the twentieth century through Gunkel to von Rad.

It would be quite an error to conclude that Bailey has cast no light on the understanding of Genesis 19. His effort to remove the sexual interpretation of Genesis 19:5 from the time of the Jahwist[26] down to the Maccabean period, nevertheless, is not persuasive.

One might assume that 943 nonsexual uses of "know" (*yadha^c*) against ten sexual uses (excepting Genesis 19:5 and Judges 19:22) prove nonsexual use in Genesis 19:5; but such is not the case. Word definitions are determined not by arithmetical frequency but by contextual meaning. In fact, according to Bailey's own criteria, *yadha^c* does occur in the sexual sense in the early, preexilic stratum of the Pentateuchal tradition, specifically at Genesis 4:1, 17, 25; 19:8; 24:16; and 38:26.[27] If the coital sense appears thus in such an early stratum, with one instance (Genesis 19:8) in the same context

---

[26] Source critics usually assign the Sodom saga to the Jahwist between 950 and 850 B.C. Robert Pfeiffer, *Introduction to the Old Testament* (New York: Harper & Bros., 1941), pp. 159–67, prefers to designate the source of Genesis 19 as "S" (for Southern or Seir). He felt it was "idle" to speculate about the date of S sources, although they must have been before 600 B.C. in his view, for this is the time at which he placed redactions (called S²) in S.

[27] Georg Fohrer, *Introduction to the Old Testament,* trans. David Green (Nashville: Abingdon Press, 1968), pp. 147, 160f., assigns all these texts either to J or N (Nomadic), both of which are preexilic. If one chooses the stratification proposed by Pfeiffer's *Introduction,* pp. 143, 160, which ascribes all the Genesis texts cited by Bailey either to J, S, or S² (only 24:16 belongs to J; only 4:25 to S²), then one still supports the sexual sense of "know" by its attestation in material of the same stratum as that embracing 19:5.

33

with the disputed verse 19:5, the probability that 19:5 belongs to the category of the ten cases rather than to that of the 943 seems more likely. We can also understand why Norman Gottwald begins his discussion of the distinctive vocabulary and style of the Jahwist material with this characterization, "'to know' as a euphemism for sexual intercourse,"[28] although Gottwald doubtlessly includes Genesis 19:5 in such a generalization. Despite Bailey's attractive argument and the possibility that any Jahwist material was subject to transmissional editing, the thrust of 19:8 is so obviously sexual that it becomes arbitrary to disconnect it from the sense of 19:5.

Bailey reinforces his argument for a nonsexual reading of Genesis 19:5 by appeal to the parallel in Judges 19:22. That is, in Josephus' *Antiquities* there is a discussion of the Sodom episode as well as the remarkable parallel at Gibeah in Judges 19. Although the two stories coincide in important details, Josephus makes no reference in his paraphrase of Judges 19:22 to pederastic or homosexual assault:

> But some of the young men of Gabah, who had seen the woman in the market place and admired her comeliness, when they learned that she lodged with the old man, scorning the feebleness of these few, came to the doors; and when the old man bade them begone and not to resort to violence and outrage, they required him to hand over his woman guest if he wished to avoid trouble. (*Ant.* V 143).

By contrast, Josephus, like Gunkel, finds at Sodom a tale involving beautiful boys. Bailey cites[29] *Antiquities* I xi 1 (194–95) and I xi 3 (200):

> About this time the Sodomites grew proud, on account of their riches and great wealth: they became unjust towards men, and impious towards God . . . , they hated strangers, and abused themselves with Sodomitical practises. God was therefore much displeased at them, and determined to punish them for their pride. . . . Now when the Sodomites saw the young men (the angels) to be of beautiful countenances, and this to an extraordinary degree . . . they resolved themselves to enjoy these beautiful boys by force and violence.

In these phrases Bailey follows the older Whiston translation.[30] In

---

[28] Norman Gottwald, *A Light to the Nations* (New York: Harper & Bros., 1959), p. 219.

[29] Bailey, *Homosexuality*, p. 23.

[30] William Whiston, trans., *The Works of Flavius Josephus*, vol. 1 (Philadelphia: J. Grigg, 1831), p. 27. McNeill, *The Church and the Homosexual*, p. 73, following Bailey, repeats this error.

the first paragraph (*Ant.* xi 1) the clause "abused themselves with Sodomitical practises" is certainly incorrect[31] and should read, with Thackeray, "hated foreigners and declined all intercourse with others."[32] Sodom's imperious xenophobia stands out. It can be noted in passing that Josephus alludes to Sodom's sumptuousness in words hauntingly close to the Sodom reference in Ezekiel 16:49. Bailey would have strengthened his case by avoiding Whiston in the first quotation (*Ant.* I xi 1), although the second one (*Ant.* I xi 3) does revert to the pederastic (beautiful boys) interpretation I have already objected to in Gunkel. It is not clear whether Gunkel derived his view from Josephus.

Bailey contends that since the pederastic interpretation is absent from Josephus in his view of Judges 19:22, the presence of that view in Josephus' understanding of Genesis 19:5 proves that the nonsexual interpretation of both passages is correct. At a time not much earlier than Josephus, the Genesis passage, under strong antihellenistic tendencies, succumbed to the pederastic explanation and eventually affected (by assimilation) the text of Judges 19.

In the following section my objective is to show from an examination of the parallel passages that Judges 19 is the earliest exposition of Genesis 19 we have, that it does sustain the sexual interpretation of "know" in Genesis 19:5, but that Josephus, for ethnic reasons, chose to repress this element in the rape at Gibeah.

JUDGES 19: EARLIEST COMMENTARY ON GENESIS 19

The critical sections of the rape at Gibeah and the attempted rape at Sodom are presented here in parallel:

	Context: Preparing to spend the night in the square, the Levite and his company are met by an old Ephraimite. The Levite says:
(Genesis 19:1–13, RSV)	(Judges 19:18–30, RSV)
¹The two angels came to Sodom	¹⁸"I went to Bethlehem in Judah;

---

[31] Seemingly, Whiston's homophobia rather than Josephus' in this instance.

[32] H. St. J. Thackeray, trans., Flavius Josephus, vol. IV, *Jewish Antiquities* (Books I–IV), Loeb Classical Library (Cambridge, MA: Harvard University Press, 1967), p. 97. The correct text, at the clause in question, reads *einai te misoxenoi kai tas pros allous homilias ektrepesthai.* The *kai* clause is explanatory. "Intercourse" (*homilia*) occurs here in the nonsexual sense.

in the evening; and Lot was sitting in the gate of Sodom. When Lot saw them, he rose to meet them, and bowed himself with his face to the earth, ²and said, "My lords, turn aside, I pray you, to your servant's house and spend the night, and wash your feet; then you may rise up early and go your way." They said, "No; we will spend the night in the street." ³But he urged them strongly; so they turned aside to him and entered his house; and he made them a feast, and baked unleavened bread, and they ate. ⁴But before they lay down, the men of the city, the men of Sodom, both young and old, all the people to the last man, surrounded the house; ⁵and they called to Lot, "Where are the men who came to you tonight? Bring them out to us, that we may know them." ⁶Lot went out of the door to the men, shut the door after him, ⁷and said, "I beg you, my brothers, do not act so wickedly. ⁸Behold, I have two daughters who have not known man; let me bring them out to you, and do to them as you please; only do nothing to these men, for they have come under the shelter of my roof." ⁹But they said, "Stand back!" And they said, "This fellow came to sojourn, and he would play the judge! Now we will deal worse with you than with them." Then they pressed hard against the man Lot, and drew near to break the door. ¹⁰But the men put forth their hands and brought Lot into the house to

and I am going to my home; and nobody takes me into his house. ¹⁹We have straw and provender for our asses, with bread and wine for me and your maidservant and the young man with your servants; there is no lack of anything." ²⁰And the old man said, "Peace be to you; I will care for all your wants; only, do not spend the night in the square." ²¹So he brought him into his house, and gave the asses provender, and they washed their feet, and ate and drank.

²²As they were making their hearts merry, behold, the men of the city, base fellows, beset the house round about, beating on the door; and they said to the old man, the master of the house, "Bring out the man who came into your house, that we may know him." ²³And the man, the master of the house, went out to them and said to them, "No, my brethren, do not act so wickedly; seeing that this man has come into my house, do not do this vile thing. ²⁴Behold, here are my virgin daughter and his concubine; let me bring them out now. Ravish them and do with them what seems good to you; but against this man do not do so vile a thing." ²⁵But the men would not listen to him. So the man seized his concubine, and put her out to them; and they knew her, and abused her all night until the morning. And as the dawn began to break, they let her go. ²⁶And as the morning appeared, the woman came and fell down at the

them, and shut the door. [11]And they struck with blindness the men who were at the door of the house, both small and great, so that they wearied themselves groping for the door. [12]Then the men said to Lot, "Have you any one else here? Sons-in-law, sons, daughters, or any one you have in the city, bring them out of the place; [13] for we are about to destroy this place, because the outcry against its people has become great before the Lord, and the Lord has sent us to destroy it."

door of the man's house where her master was, till it was light.

[27]And her master rose up in the morning, and when he opened the doors of the house and went out to go on his way, behold, there was his concubine lying at the door of the house, with her hands on the threshold. [28]He said to her, "Get up, let us be going." But there was no answer. Then he put her upon the ass; and the man rose up and went away to his home. [29]And when he entered his house, he took a knife, and laying hold of his concubine he divided her, limb by limb, into twelve pieces, and sent her throughout all the territory of Israel. [30]And all who saw it said, "Such a thing has never happened or been seen from the day that the people of Israel came up out of the land of Egypt until this day; consider it, take counsel, and speak."

The striking points of specific parallel may be singled out as follows:

Genesis 19:2: Spend the night in the street.

Judges 19:15, 20: Spend the night in the square.

Genesis 19: Grossly inhospitable city; single hospitable good man, himself a resident alien (vs. 9).

Judges 19: Grossly inhospitable city; single hospitable good man, himself a resident alien (vs. 16).

Genesis 19:4: Wicked men of Sodom surround the host's house.

Judges 19:22: Base fellows of Gibeah beset the host's house round about.

Genesis 19:5: They want to womanize the two guests.

Judges 19:22: They want to womanize the Levite.

Genesis 19:7–8: Host offers two virgin daughters.	Judges 19:24: Host offers virgin daughter and Levite's concubine.

The extent of these parallels demands some kind of explanation. A substantial group of authorities, of whom W. Nowack,[33] following Karl Budde,[34] is a good example, find the Gibeah tradition in Judges 19 subsequently edited to conform more closely to the Sodom account. Nowack points out that the Levite in Judges 20:5 says nothing about a homosexual attack: "And the men of Gibeah rose against me, and beset the house round about me by night; they meant to kill me, and they ravished my concubine, and she is dead." Furthermore, the host would hardly have risked allowing the Levite to expose himself (vs. 25) to these men; nor would they have contented themselves with the Levite's concubine alone (vs. 25) after refusing both the concubine and the host's virgin daughter.

Nowack and Budde go on to affirm that the correct solution to these difficulties is to assume that Judges 19:22 said nothing about knowing the Levite, but only his concubine. So Nowack emends the text as follows:

> [22] As they were making merry, behold, the people of the city, good-for-nothing fellows, surrounded the house, beating against the door, and they said to the old man, the master of the house, "Bring out the woman who has come into the house, that we may know her." [23] Then the man, the master of the house, went out to them and said to them, "No, my brethren, do not act wickedly! Since this man has come into my house, do not commit this crime! [24] Here is my virgin daughter; I will bring her out; ravish her and do with her as you please, but do not venture to do such a wicked deed to this man. [25] But the men were not willing to listen to him. The man then seized his concubine and brought her out to them, and they knew her and worked their wantonness on her the entire night until morning; then, as dawn broke, they let her go.[35]

[33] W. Nowack, *Richter, Ruth und Bücher Samuelis*, Handkommentar zum Alten Testament (Göttingen: Vandenhoeck & Ruprecht, 1902), p. 164.

[34] Karl Budde, *Das Buch der Richter*, Kurzer Hand-Kommentar zum Alten Testament (Tübingen: J.C.B. Mohr, 1897), p. 131. C.F. Burney, *The Book of Judges*, 2d ed. (London: Rivingtons, 1930), pp. 444f., lays out the verbal parallels interestingly, declaring them to be "deliberately modelled." J. Alberto Soggin, *Judges*, trans. John Bowden, Old Testament Library (Philadelphia: Westminster Press, 1981), p. 282, finds Judges 19 considerably dependent on Genesis 19.

[35] Nowack, *Richter*, pp. 164f.

This translation would conform to Bailey's analysis of the Gibeah tradition based on emphases in Josephus (i.e., the absence of homosexual attack in vs. 22). *The New English Bible* refers similarly in verse 24 only to the old man's virgin daughter but does not yield to this emendation at verse 22.

These revisions were considered in detail by George F. Moore[36] in 1895 and were rejected because of Judges 20:5. That is, the threat of rape might have been represented by the Levite as an attempt on his very life, whereas the proposed reconstruction of verse 22 would leave "nothing in chapter 19 to intimate that the man was in any way molested or threatened, and 20:5 is left without any foundation." Elimination of the danger of homosexual attack in Judges 19:22, therefore, would also seem to require the removal or radical emendation of 20:5. One may conclude, therefore, that Judges 19:22 resists the effort to erase its verbal similarity to Genesis 19:5 and that both texts use "know" in the sexual sense of male on male.

The late dating of Judges 19—21 is generally accepted, even if the redactor of the material has made use of the Jahwist tradition from the ninth or tenth century B.C. Moore, for example, summarizes the complexity of sources in Judges[37] and finds these chapters marked by postexilic (i.e., after 538 B.C.) features. Otto Eissfeldt also finds nuances and influences of the priestly tradition, which is postexilic.[38] Robert Boling criticizes Moore for putting the final redactor in the fourth century B.C. but places his work back only so far as the exile itself.[39] It seems probable, therefore, that the Gibeah rape story, despite its Jahwist features, reflects the Genesis parallel in a secondary manner. According to a recognized scribal tendency (assimilation) to expand points of agreement in such parallels, elements like the two women (instead of one, vs. 25) may well reflect this assimilation. But verse 22 confirms the sexual interpretation of Genesis 19:5 well before Bailey's proposed second-century B.C. origin of that interpretation.

It remains now to ask why Josephus avoids in the Gibeah episode the same-sex theme he confirms in its Genesis counterpart. To get

[36] G. F. Moore, *Judges*, International Critical Commentary, 7th ed. (Edinburgh: T & T Clark, 1895; 1958), pp. 417f.
[37] Ibid., pp. xxxiii–vi.
[38] Otto Eissfeldt, *The Old Testament: An Introduction*, trans. Peter R. Ackroyd (New York: Harper & Row, 1965), p. 267.
[39] Robert G. Boling, *Judges*, The Anchor Bible (Garden City, NY: Doubleday, 1975), p. 278.

the flavor of Josephus' viewpoint, we return to Judges 20:5, in which the Levite, after saving his own neck at the cost of the concubine's life, confirms the worst that women have said of patriarchy by evoking pity over his own plight at Gibeah and effectively removing from the report his own throwing of the concubine to the mercy of the rapists ("they meant to kill me, and they ravished my concubine, and she is dead"). This is on a moral par with 1 Timothy 2:14. "And Adam was not deceived, but the woman was deceived and became a transgressor." The Levite's own account of the event, however, is a model of masculine bravery by comparison with Josephus' report, which goes like this:

> Driven to such a pass and unwilling to suffer his guests to be abused, he offered the men his own daughter, declaring that it would be more legitimate for them thus to gratify their lust than by doing violence to his guests, and for his part thinking by this means to avoid wronging those whom he had received. But they in no wise abated their passion for the stranger, being insistent in their demands to have her, and while he was yet imploring them to perpetrate no iniquity, they seized the woman and, yielding still more to the force of their lust, carried her off to their homes and then, after sating their lewdness all night long, let her go towards the break of day. She, outworn with her woes, repaired to the house of her host, where, out of grief at what she had endured and not daring for shame to face her husband—since he above all, she deemed, would be inconsolable at her fate—she succumbed and gave up the ghost. But her husband, supposing his wife to be buried in deep sleep and suspecting nothing serious, tried to rouse her, with intent to console her by recalling how she had not voluntarily surrendered herself to her abusers, but that they had come to the lodginghouse and carried her off.[40]

Thackeray footnotes with marked understatement the fact that "in Scripture, the Levite himself surrenders the woman."[41] If Josephus' description of the Levite's conduct toward his concubine markedly increases the element of chauvinism already present in the biblical account, is there a kindred tendency at work that would induce him to subtract from the script of the Gibeah "hell-raisers"[42] their intent to commit sexual rape of the Levite? The following considerations encourage a positive answer to this question.

First, Gibeah remained a city of Benjaminites, part of the cove-

[40]Josephus, *Ant.* V 145–48.
[41]Thackeray, trans., Josephus, *Ant.* 4, p. 69, n. a.
[42]Boling, *Judges*, p. 276.

nantal league of Israel (Judges 19:12, 16). The object of the final editing of Judges, with its preview in chapter 1 and postview in chapters 19—21, was to confirm a people broken by the experience of defeat and exile by recalling that in days of old, before there was a king, the nation had endured chaos and, through blood, sweat, and tears, had found divine deliverance and restoration of national solidarity. After the bitter disappointments of the First Jewish Revolt against Rome, Josephus is well positioned to appreciate the message that Judges is designed to teach.

Following the incredible massacre of the Benjaminites in chapter 20 for their treatment of the Levite's concubine,[43] not only are the Benjaminites restored to covenantal unity with the offended majority (chap. 21), but Jabesh-gilead's resistance of the draft for the war against Benjamin is also punished by a grand rip-off of its daughters to supply brides for the newly reconciled but wifeless Benjaminites.

We have already seen that Josephus finds in Sodom an example of Greek pederasty. This practice characterizes pagan idolators like Greeks or Sodomites, Canaanites or Syrians, but not the sons of Abraham, who the Benjaminites, despite everything, remain. So Josephus, prompted by ethnic loyalty as he writes for pagan Roman readership, emends the story at verse 22, just as he fictionalizes on both masculine *and* sacerdotal grounds the conduct of the Levite.

Second, Saul, the first king, was a man of Gibeah (1 Samuel 10:26; 11:4, etc.). Is Josephus' redaction together with an altered chronology that places the Gibeah scandal after chapter 2 designed[44] to distance the emergence of the first king from the shameless conduct of his compatriots?

Third, Sodom received for its wrongdoing fire and brimstone, extinction to the last man (sic). It would be partial of God to impose, in wrath, so severe a penalty in the first case while avoiding it in the second. This persuades Josephus, then, to turn aside from the line of thought he has already established in respect to Genesis 19:5 when he comes to its obvious echo in the case of Gibeah.

Finally, a significant parallel to the editorial proclivity of Josephus can be adduced from the Greek version of the Old Testament. In the

---

[43]The battles of chapter 20 are depicted in the style of Cecil B. De Mille or the fictitious schematization of the Qumran War Scroll. It is difficult to concur in Boling's criticism (ibid., p. 278) of Moore for finding in Judges decline in historical and even religious authenticity.

[44]Cf. Coleman, *Christian Attitudes to Homosexuality*, p. 84.

41

Hebrew scriptures it is clear that Canaanite cultic practices, including both female and male cultic prostitution, were assimilated into Hebrew religion. Tamar (Genesis 38:21–23) is called by the term (q*e*deshah) applied to the female cult prostitute. Male cult prostitutes (qad*e*shim) are specifically mentioned in 1 Kings 14:24 under Rehoboam. They are chased out by Asa (1 Kings 15:12) and again by Jehoshaphat (1 Kings 22:46). More than two centuries later Josiah's attack (2 Kings 23:7) shows that they were still there and that sacred prostitution had become attached to the temple cultus itself. Representing a later priestly revision, the Chronicler makes no reference to it in the parallel passages, and this tendency is carried out on a grand scale in the Septuagint. The translators avoid the term for cultic prostitute altogether, with the single exception of a transliteration (kādesim) of the Hebrew at 2 Kings 23:7, incomprehensible to a Greek reader unfamiliar with Hebrew. At Genesis 38:21 and Deuteronomy 23:17, for example, they use the word for secular prostitute (pornē, pornos). This "transforms the prohibition of cultic prostitution into a prohibition of licentiousness in general."[45] They avoid the logical Greek word for sacred prostitute, hierodoulos, where the Hebrew counterpart (qadesh) occurs. Asa does not purge the qad*e*shim (1 Kings 15:12), but the "festal rites" (hai teletai). From this and additional evidence Friedrich Hauck and Siegfried Schulz conclude that within the Septuagint "the reader finds no express mention at all of cultic prostitution in Israel."[46] Josephus' alterations of the Gibeah tradition replicate in a specific case what is done in the Septuagint programmatically, for reasons that are similar, if not identical, in detail.

PHALLIC AGGRESSION AND THE PROPHETIC CRY FOR JUSTICE

The foregoing discussion has shown that Gunkel's discovery of attempted pederastic rape on the part of the men and boys of Sodom reads into the biblical record ideas based on nineteenth-century Judeo-Christian revulsion for Greek paiderastia. Sherwin Bailey's attempt, however, to read out the coital sense of "know" in Genesis 19:5 has been faulted for disregarding the tendentiousness in

---

[45] Friedrich Hauck and Siegfried Schulz, "pornē," "pornos," ktl., *Theological Dictionary of the New Testament*, ed. G. Friedrich, trans. and ed. G.W. Bromiley (Grand Rapids, MI: Wm. B. Eerdmans, 1968), 6:586.
[46] Ibid.

Josephus' handling of the parallel to Genesis 19:5 in Judges 19:22 and the contextual meaning of Genesis 19:5 itself. Now the positive, liberationist results of these criticisms must be brought out.

The "outcry" against Sodom of Genesis 18:21 is expressed by a technical legal term *(z^ec^aqa)* signifying "the cry for help which one who suffers great injustice screams."[47] This is the outcry against violence *(hamas)* voiced by the prophet Jeremiah on behalf of the poor (Jeremiah 22:13–17) and on his own behalf in the oppression he experiences by taking up the cause of the oppressed (Jeremiah 20:8). This recurrent prophetic outcry against violent injustice done by the rich to the poor is based not only in the remembrance of Israel's own bondage/deliverance (Exodus 3) but also in its role as alien and wanderer (Deuteronomy 26:5).

In his monumental work on *The Tribes of Jahweh,* Norman Gottwald has given these central themes of prophetic preachment extensive sociological undergirding by locating the history of Hebrew beginnings in "the successful convergence of several antistatist sectors of the populace in imperial-feudal Canaanite societies of the fourteenth to thirteenth centuries B.C."[48] Gottwald persuasively argues that the component elements of this early confederation were the following: mercenary warriors *(^capiru* in the Amarna letters); the agricultural and pastoral brigands called *Shoshu,* who resisted Egyptian hegemony, especially in southern Edom; restive peasants *(hupshu)* remote to the urban centers as well as those "working on feudal latifundia under the direct control of the urban aristocracy."[49] On Gottwald's terms the conquest of Canaan is not to be seen as a massive incursion from the outside by Exodus Israelites from Egypt. These invaders were only a small group of lower classes revolting against oppression by the Egyptian crown[50] who linked up with much larger numbers of indigenous oppressed within Canaan, consisting of the three subgroups already mentioned. The cult of

[47]Von Rad, *Genesis,* p. 211.
[48]Norman K. Gottwald, *The Tribes of Yahweh: A Sociology of the Religion of Liberated Israel, 1250–1050 B.C.* (Maryknoll, NY: Orbis Books, 1979), p. xxiii. Georg Fohrer, *History of Israelite Religion,* trans. David Green (Nashville: Abingdon Press, 1973), pp. 29f., describes the *Apiru (Hapiru)* as "persons without family status . . . mercenaries, captives, slaves, foreigners of illegal status within a kingdom. The Hebrew expression '^cibri,' which is connected with this term, characterizes the early Israelites as alien groups of inferior legal status."
[49]Gottwald, *Tribes,* p. 480.
[50]Ibid., p. 455.

Jahweh brought into Canaan by the Exodus Levites[51] absorbed and transformed attributes of the Canaanite El God as the deity of an emergent antifeudal order in Canaan. Prophetic Jahwism receives from this sociological heritage a network of revolutionary roots in marginated and exploited sectors of the Egyptian empire. The prophetic demand of justice for the poor and protection of the homeless alien sustains the character of moral and political concern that informs the origins of Hebrew religion and sees in Sodom the epitome of disregard for the rights of the powerless that characterized Canaanite statism.

Josephus (*Ant. I xi 1* [194–95]) retains the specific ingredients of the prophetic heritage in his outcry against the arrogant wealth of Sodom and its "hatred of strangers." The city's xenophobia is directly linked with its jealous protectiveness toward its own secure affluence. Aside from his own culturally induced anathema on Sodom's alleged *paiderastia*, Josephus' perception of the matter is profoundly kin to Ezekiel's judgment centuries before: "Behold, this was the guilt of your sister Sodom: she and her daughters[52] had pride, surfeit of food, and prosperous ease, but did not aid the poor and needy [Ezek. 16:49]." Struck by the unique description of Sodom's delinquency in this text, Walter Eichrodt comments:

> Here . . . Jerusalem is regarded as having sunk far lower than Sodom, whose sin is described not as the shameless perversity of Gen. 19 but as the godless self-security of a rich worldly city, which adds to its hybris a hard unsympathizing attitude toward those menaced by hunger and want, thus drawing down Jahweh's wrath and judgment upon itself. This characterization of Sodom is so audacious as to raise the question whether it does not presuppose a different tradition about the destruction of Sodom from the one in Gen. 19.[53]

Eichrodt's question about "a different tradition" is not answerable solely on grounds of source or tradition criticism. The text must be approached in a new way. The reader must put aside pious heterosexual anathemas on private, voluntary, same-sex acts by homosexually predisposed adults. The key is the violent, aggressive abuse of power that had already brought on the city the outcry of "foul play"

---

[51] Ibid., p. 496.

[52] Sodom's gender on the sin side looks feminine to the prophet, as in the case of Hosea's miscreant wife.

[53] Walter Eichrodt, *Ezekiel: A Commentary*, trans. Crosslett Quinn, Old Testament Library (Philadelphia: Westminster Press, 1970), p. 108.

(ḥamas) long before the advent of the divine emissaries in Genesis 19. This mode of interpretation is substantiated in the tradition of Jesus.

It is a major impediment to those who wish to use scripture as a cudgel against homosexual persons to deny them membership or office in the community of faith that the teaching of Jesus contains no reference to homosexual disposition or acts. But Sodom does appear briefly in this tradition—twice in Matthew at 10:15 (Sodom and Gomorrah) and 11:24 (Sodom) and once in Luke at 10:12 (Sodom). Two of these (Matthew 10:15 and Luke 10:12) are in settings of a charge, or commissioning, of apostles. Matthew 11:24 occurs in connection with the woe pronounced on Chorazin, Bethsaida, and Capernaum, for their imperviousness to the message and work of Jesus. The one Lucan text is sufficient for our purpose and reads as follows in its context:

> [10] When you enter a town and they do not make you welcome, go out into its streets and say, [11] "The very dust of your town that clings to our feet we wipe off to your shame. Only take note of this: the kingdom of God has come close." [12] I tell you, it will be more bearable for Sodom on the great Day than for that town [NEB].

The saying on Sodom's demise appears to have been an independent fragment of Q (material common to Matthew and Luke but lacking in Mark), which Luke attached to the sending out of the seventy and which Matthew joined to the woe pronounced on unreceptive Galilean towns. The singular fact is that this saying, in all three of its occurrences, sets Sodom's doom in the context of inhospitality to the representatives of Jesus or to Jesus himself. This is consonant with the underlying motif of the spurning of divine representatives ascribed by Gunkel to Genesis 19 on the basis of history-of-religions methodology. It accords with the requirement to defend the alien and dispossessed arising from sociological criticism of the period of the conquest (1250–1050 B.C.) and the deepest historical roots of the word Hebrew. It accommodates without exegetical coercion the sexual interpretation of Genesis 19:5 by its stringent repudiation of the phallic aggression represented in that text.

This interpretation liberates the text from the oppressive use it has so long served in our religious history and enables the reader (gay/lesbian or straight) to enter into the striving after justice that is the heart of prophetic faith and the soul of evangelical freedom.

Only on the basis of such exegesis can the Judeo-Christian tradition renovate its social ministry in the world by a responsible (i.e., charitable) use of power, solidarity with the alien and poor, the doing of justice informed by love.

I have already alluded to Kenneth Dover's reminder that "human societies at many times and in many regions have subjected strangers, newcomers and trespassers to homosexual anal violation as a way of reminding them of their subordinate status."[54] Dover goes on in the same context to discuss the Greek god Priapos, guardian of orchards and gardens. He is "represented as having a massive penis in a state of readiness to penetrate a thief of either sex."[55] Dover also describes one Attic red-figure vase that pictures the theme of phallic conquest in the following manner:

> A man in Persian costume, informing us, "I am Eurymedon. I stand bent over," suits his posture to his words, while a Greek, half-erect penis in hand, strides toward him with an arresting gesture. This expresses the exultation of the "manly" Athenians at their victory over the "womanish" Persians at the river Eurymedon in the early 460s, it proclaims, "We've buggered the Persians!"[56]

Because the saga of Genesis 19 has no recognizable cultic elements to encourage the opinion of some commentators that it is Canaanite cultic prostitution which is under attack in the depiction of the men of Sodom, the practice of phallic aggression, in the larger setting of opulent, xenophobic hybris, underlined by Ezekiel and Josephus, provides the most logical explanation of the sexual dimension of Genesis 19. This specific understanding leads Thorkil Vanggaard to affirm that "the aggressive element, void of all eroticism, is precisely what is operating in such scenes of collective violence as that described in the biblical tale of Sodom."[57] It should be self-evident that the healthy homosexual would no more condone the conduct implicit in Genesis 19:5 than the healthy heterosexual would approve the conduct of Judges 19:22–25.

[54] Dover, *Greek Homosexuality,* p. 105.
[55] Ibid., p. 150.
[56] Ibid.
[57] Thorkil Vanggaard, *Phallós: A Symbol and Its History in the Male World,* trans. Thorkil Vanggaard (London: Jonathan Cape, 1972), p. 102.

CHAPTER/THREE

Sodom Among the Prophets

Because of the importance of the prophets in the rise of ethical monotheism and the pivotal function of prophecy in the justice of God as comprehended in liberation theology, I propose now to project on the wider prophetic screen what has been said about Ezekiel 16:49 in Chapter Two.

The argument proceeds on the following lines. Despite opposition to Baalism in the prophetic and Deuteronomic tradition, references to male cultic prostitution are significantly infrequent. In no instance does a prophet ascribe either the destruction of Sodom or the impending demise of Israel and Judah to homosexual activity. The distinctiveness of the prophetic view can be made evident over against the Deuteronomist and the Holiness Code (Leviticus 17—26) by examination of the occurrences of "abominations" *(to^{c}eboth)* and (male) "cult prostitutes" *(q^{e}deshim)*. The prophetic emphasis on the justice of God provides a much more profound view of the character and consequences of human wrongdoing than do Levitical ideas of holiness, which have permitted so many religious people to see in "sodomy" (i.e., acts of oral or anal intercourse between males[1]) the quintessential and proximate cause of God's destructive wrath.

[1] If the definition of "sodomy" is controlled by the historical exegesis of the account in Genesis 19, it would probably mean coercive anal intercourse between males. Popular and legal usage has, over time, given the word such diverse implications that one must ask each user of it what specifically is meant. *Webster's Ninth New Collegiate Dictionary*, ed. F.C. Mish and others (Springfield, MA: Merriam-Webster, 1983), p. 1120, provides an example of this diversity in two meanings: "1. copulation with a member of the same sex or with an animal. 2. noncoital and esp. anal or oral copulation with a member of the opposite sex." Even the first part of 1. is removed from Genesis 19 in its inattention to the element of coercion.

THE DESTRUCTION OF SODOM AND THE FALL OF NATIONS

The second part of the Hebrew canon—the Former Prophets—comprises Joshua, Judges, Samuel, and Kings. Consisting mainly of historical narration, with the book of Deuteronomy serving as a legislative introduction to the whole, this material tells how Hebrew kings, according to prophetic standards of judgment, brought the nation by obedience toward life, by disobedience toward death. Peter Coleman summarizes current opinion on the Deuteronomic history (Deuteronomy plus the Former Prophets) as follows:

> The "history" is characterized by a theological premise that the decline and fall of the two kingdoms of Israel and Judah have to be explained, not by the weakness of the people before their invaders, but as a demonstration of the power and judgement of God on their disobedience. This premise is in a sense nothing other than the message of the major prophets, particularly Amos, but it is expressed in the Deuteronomistic corpus both in terms of the laws that should have been obeyed and in comment on the kings who are assessed in terms of their righteousness before God, rather than from the political or economic success of their reigns.[2]

As might be expected on the basis of this characterization, within the Deuteronomic history and the prophets generally, references do occur to Sodom as a symbol of moral reprobation and frightful judgment suffered as a result of it. Gomorrah is at times linked to Sodom, although Genesis tells nothing of Gomorrah's misdeeds.[3] Explicit Old Testament references to Sodom outside the context of Genesis 19 are the following: Deuteronomy 29:23; 32:32; Isaiah 1:9–10; 3:9; 13:19; Jeremiah 23:14; 49:18; 50:40; Lamentations 4:6; Ezekiel 16:46–56; Amos 4:11; Zephaniah 2:9.[4] If popular exegesis of Genesis 19 were correct, we could expect these passages to specify sodomy as a conspicuous cause of national doom. Contextual examination, however, yields the following conclusions.

Deuteronomy 29 contains summary admonitions of Moses to

[2]Peter Coleman, *Christian Attitudes to Homosexuality* (London: SPCK, 1980), pp. 39f.

[3]Gerhard von Rad, *Genesis: A Commentary*, 3d Eng. ed., trans. John H. Marks, Old Testament Library (Philadelphia: Westminster Press, 1972), p. 221, holds that the words "and Gomorrah" in Genesis 18:20; 19:24f., 28 are editorial additions. The five cities of the valley of Sittim or Salt Sea (Genesis 14:2f.) consumed by fire, according to Wisdom 10:6, are named in Genesis 14:2, 8 as Sodom, Gomorrah, Admah, Zeboiim, Bela (or Zoar). How Zoar as Lot's refuge (Genesis 19:22f.) is also destroyed remains unexplained. Cf. Deuteronomy 29:23.

[4]For nonexplicit references to Sodom, see n. 9.

stand fast in the covenant of Deuteronomic law (vss. 9, 25) and to disdain the gentile gods (vss. 16–18). Failure to do so will bring down the desolating curses of the covenant (vs. 21), resulting in a land reduced to brimstone, salt, and burning, like Sodom, Gomorrah, Admah, and Zeboiim (vs. 23). The cause of this doom is also stated: abandonment of the covenant (vs. 25), devotion to other gods (vs. 26). It is correct that Deuteronomy 23:17 legislates against the female and the male cult prostitute, but this has no discernible connection with Sodom either in Genesis or in Deuteronomy, and the covenant of law enjoined by Moses contains numerous injunctions on an undifferentiated par with 23:17, such as abstinence from pork because swine have cleft hooves and do not chew the cud (14:8); the stoning to death of a disobedient son (21:18–21); and the prohibition of clothing made from mingled wool and linen (22:11).

Deuteronomy 32:32 stands in a final song of Moses (32:1–43). Verse 32 in context accents the fierce retribution of God the Rock (vs. 30), who despoils the produce of heathen adversaries like the vine of Sodom and the fields of Gomorrah. This reveals only that pagan Sodom was laid waste. Homosexual acts as the cause of this desolation are as remote to 32:32 as they are to 29:23. Deuteronomy contains many rich and enduring moral insights shaped by prophetic understanding, but the modern interpreter must not assume that these are reached by a reading of the text uninstructed by sociological criticism.

Isaiah 1:9f. (eighth century B.C.) is a prophecy against Judah for sin described in terms of cultic events, sacrifices and feasts that are not backed up by justice, defense of the fatherless and widows (1:17)—recognizable ingredients of mainline prophetic proclamation. Only a handful of the faithful (1:9) separate Zion from the fate of Sodom and Gomorrah. In fact, the rulers of Judah are "rulers of Sodom" over "people of Gomorrah." Isaiah 3 continues an oracle of judgment against a Judah plagued by a state of anarchy. The prophet laments: "Their partiality witnesses against them; they proclaim their sin like Sodom, they do not hide it [3:9]." The meaning of the Hebrew is obscure, however, and may mean "the expression of their faces witnesses against them." But at 3:14f. the elders and princes are scored for despoiling the indigent and crushing God's people by "grinding the face of the poor." Isaiah 13 is an oracle against Babylon—critics assign the material to the sixth century B.C.— presumably for its ruthless aggressions against its neighbors suggested in 13:11 and 14:6. Babylon's splendor and pride will be cast down like Sodom and Gomorrah, according to Isaiah 13:19, but once again, as in the other Isaiah references to Sodom, nothing is said about same-sex activity, cultic or otherwise.

Jeremiah (seventh to sixth centuries B.C.) follows the pattern of Isaiah. The prophets of Jerusalem have "become like Sodom" (Jeremiah 23:14), but their vice consists of adultery, lying, and strengthening the hands of evildoers. Jeremiah 49:18 denounces Edom, presumably for its incursion into southern Judah after 587 B.C.,[5] by contrast with friendship for Edom commanded in Deuteronomy 23:7. Unless it be Edom's alliance with Babylon, the specific cause for likening its retribution to Sodom and Gomorrah does not sound through the loud notes of doom voiced by the prophet. In an oracle denouncing Babylon and prophesying its demise, presumably for taking Judah captive (Jeremiah 50:33), the impending destruction of the city will be comparable to the overthrow of Sodom and Gomorrah (Jeremiah 50:40).

Lamentations 4:6 and Zephaniah 2:9 also use Sodom as symbol of desolating judgment, in the first case a dirge over the city of Jerusalem laid waste by the Babylonians and in the second, a destruction on Moab and Ammon because of their chauvinism (cf. Isaiah 16:6f.) and enmity to the people of God (Zephaniah 2:10). Amos 4:11 is a passing reference to the chastisement awaiting Israel, as severe as that on Sodom and Gomorrah, but followed by divine rescue. Neither punishment nor pity has brought real repentance. Amos, a prophet of the eighth century B.C., declaimed against Israel's oppression of the poor, immorality, and ceremonial practice divorced from interhuman justice, especially in economic affairs. Passages like Amos 2:6–8 and 5:21–24 are, understandably, centerpieces of liberation theology literature. Some writers have found in Amos 2:7 ("a man and his father go in to the same maiden, so that my holy name is profaned") a suggestion of cultic prostitution,[6] but the noun for female cult prostitute (*q^edesha*) does not appear in this verse, and the trend against this interpretation has been noted by James Ward.[7] Robert Coote has suggested an alternative view, faithful to the context, that drops the sexual meaning entirely and finds

[5]Cf. John Bright, *Jeremiah*, The Anchor Bible (New York: Doubleday, 1965), pp. 331–32.

[6]Cf. Artur Weiser, *Das Buch der zwölf kleinen Propheten*, Bd. 1, 6. Aufl., Alte Testament Deutsch (Göttingen: Vandenhoeck & Ruprecht, 1974), p. 141.

[7]James M. Ward, *Amos and Isaiah* (Nashville: Abingdon Press, 1969), p. 136, where bibliography against the cultic prostitution viewpoint is found.

in "the maiden"—the Hebrew does not use the word same, which derives from the Greek version—a barmaid (or alewife) who gives loans at exorbitant rates.[8] In the Amos setting this may refer to the plight of the borrowers or the unjust delight of the usurious lenders behind the barmaid.

None of these passages, directly from the prophets, violates what we have previously seen in the case of Ezekiel 16:49, in which arrogance, sumptuousness, and oppression of the poor (with no mention of the sin that is said to have made Sodom famous) are the bases of the impending catastrophe. It must also be affirmed that the evidence of these texts does not add up to a mere argument from silence, because the prophets in virtually every instance (like Ezekiel 16:49) provide an agenda of grievances adequately specific to justify the doom to come. This is also borne out in a number of references not explicitly naming Sodom: Psalm 11:6; 140:10; Job 18:15; Isaiah 34:9; Jeremiah 20:16; Ezekiel 38:22; and Hosea 11:8.[9]

ABOMINATIONS IN EZEKIEL AND THE HOLINESS CODE

The whole of Ezekiel 16 is overlaid with sexual motifs constructed from the androcentric viewpoint. Verses 1–43, not unlike Hosea 2,

[8] Robert B. Coote, *Amos Among the Prophets* (Philadelphia: Fortress Press, 1981), pp. 35–36. It may be added to Coote's remarks that the Hebrew expression "go into a woman," in the sexual sense, is usually expressed with the phrase *boʾ ʿel*, but in this case we find *halak ʾel*. If the sexual sense is required at Amos 2:7, it is the only instance in the Old Testament in which *halak* is so used. See W. Gesenius, *A Hebrew and English Lexicon of the Old Testament*, ed., F. Brown, S.R. Driver, and C.A. Briggs (Oxford: Clarendon Press, 1952), p. 231.

[9] Psalm 11:6 mentions "fire and brimstone." Verse 5 specifies wickedness as love of violence (Hebrew *ḥamas*). If the "burning coals" of Psalm 140:10 refer to Sodom, standard prophetic judgments surround the meaning of the psalm: the speaking of evil, violent aggression, and God's defense of the cause of the needy (vs. 12). Job 18:15 (in a speech of Bildad) alludes to brimstone among the numerous misfortunes of the wicked, but Job is not accused of sodomy and finds the counsel of Bildad vacuous anyway (chap. 19). Brimstone also enters the apocalyptic judgment scene of Isaiah 34:9, as part of a relentless retribution against the goyim because, presumably, of aggression against Israel. Jeremiah 20:16 is a woe on the one who announces Jeremiah's birth; such a one should suffer the fate of "the cities which the Lord overthrew." Ezekiel 38:22 prophesies fire and brimstone as part of doom on Gog, the instrument of doom on Israel. Hosea 11:8 speaks only of Almah and Zeboiim (see n. 3). The destruction of the two cities is forsworn by God (11:9). The crimes of the cities are not specified, but the whoredom and lewdness of Hosea 2; 4:10ff.; 5:3ff. are set in heterosexual frameworks. Whereas the female cult prostitute is mentioned at Hosea 4:14, the male counterpart is not named. The great plea for mercy (not sacrifice) and knowledge of God (more than burnt offerings) found at Hosea 6:6 is reexpressed in Matthew 9:13 and 12:7. It is, morally speaking, the ontological basis of the liberationist hermeneutic. See also n. 38.

51

develop the metaphor of Jerusalem as unfaithful wife. The remainder of the chapter carries the theme still further in the three sisters allegory: Jerusalem is more wicked than either her older sister Samaria or her younger sister Sodom. In verses 49-50 the vices of Sodom, previously scrutinized, are linked to "abominable things": "Behold, this was the guilt of your sister Sodom: she and her daughters had pride, surfeit of food, and prosperous ease, but did not aid the poor and needy. They were haughty, and did abominable things before me; therefore I removed them, when I saw it." The noun *to^{c}eboth*, rendered "abominable things" in Ezekiel 16:50, is a technical term also found in the two explicit proscriptions of same-sex conduct found in Leviticus 18:22 and 20:13:

> You shall not lie with a male as with a woman;
> it is an abomination.

> If a man lies with a male as with a woman,
> both of them have committed an abomination;
> they shall be put to death.

The suggestion readily follows[10] that this technical term connected with same-sex intercourse in Leviticus automatically conveys the same meaning in Ezekiel. Ezekiel's use of *to^{c}eba* (abomination) does not, we affirm, substantiate this claim. An examination of all occurrences of *to^{c}eba* and the determination of its specific contextual significance produces the following conclusions.

There are forty-three uses of "abomination" or "abominations" in Ezekiel. In all the Old Testament the word occurs 116 times. Thus Ezekiel (and/or its redactors) accounts for more than one-third of the total uses, an indication of its special importance to the prophet's vocabulary. A majority of these forty-three uses in Ezekiel are nondescript. For example, Ezekiel 5:9 inveighs against Jerusalem's violation of God's ordinances (5:7), affirming: "And because of all your abominations I will do with you what I have never yet done, and the like of which I will never do again." Because the context does not make clear which ordinances have been violated, the specific content of the abominations is not certain from this text. For the interpreter to say in such a situation, "Ah, but we already know what these abominations are from Leviticus 18:22 and 20:13," is to perceive inaccurately what Ezekiel says.

[10]Cf. Hermann Gunkel, *Genesis*, 4. Aufl., Göttinger Handkommentar zum Alten Testament (Göttingen: Vandenhoeck & Ruprecht, 1910), p. 108.

Of the forty-three instances, however, fifteen show that the probable meaning of abominations in Ezekiel is idolatry. These are 6:9, 11; 7:20; 8:6 (twice), 9, 13, 15, 17; 14:6; 16:36 (Hebrew); 18:12, 13; 20:4; 22:2.[11] This opinion is based on the context surrounding each occurrence, with acknowledgment that readers do not always read contexts in exactly the same manner. The student of Ezekiel should not be content with anything less than a careful contextual examination of all the passages in question, but these few examples provide sufficient illustration of the manner in which the conclusion has been reached that by *to^{c}eboth* the prophet means idolatry.

Ezekiel 6:1–7 prophesies against the mountains of Israel as high places on which (6:4f.) idols have been erected and altars used. Verses 6:9 and 6:11 seem to carry out the same idea, giving specific content to the abominations denounced in each case as the basis for the desolating judgment to come. Verse 7:20 explicitly joins images and abomination in adjectival relation—"abominable images." Ezekiel 8 is a visionary experience in which the prophet is brought to Jerusalem to look into the house of the Lord to see (8:6) abominations in the sanctuary. This inspection (8:10) exposes to the seer "all the idols of the house of Israel," supporting the impression encouraged by allusions to the image of jealousy at verses 4 and 5,[12] Tammuz at verse 14, and sun worship at verse 16, that all occurrences of abomination in Ezekiel 8 refer to idolatry. The next example, Ezekiel 14:6, places idols and abominations in synonymous parallelism. Ezekiel 16:36 (like 7:20) places abominations in adjectival relation to idols. Ezekiel 16 uses *to^{c}eba* nine times. The entire chapter is an extended androcentric metaphor or allegory in which the prophet describes the harlotry of Jerusalem and her daughters as worse than the abominations of her two sisters, Samaria and Sodom, together with their daughters. The whole of this chapter is thus erected on a pervasive symbolism of sexual wrongdoing, but in no instance does this symbolism pass over from parameters of heterosexual into homosexual categories. This happens in spite of enlisting Sodom and "her daughters" as one of the allegorical components. Not only is Ezekiel consistent therefore with the premise

---

[11] Remaining instances are in 5:9, 11; 7:3, 4, 8, 9; 9:4; 11:18, 21; 12:16; 16:2, *22*, *43*, *47*, *50*, *51* (twice), *58*; 18:24; *22:11*; *23:36*; *33:26*; 36:31; 43:8; 44:6, 7, 13. Those italicized are occurrences in which the abomination, either literally or figuratively, is expressed in terms of heterosexual sin, but not sodomy.

[12] Cf. the parallelism of Deuteronomy 32:16.

that no prophet adduces sodomy as the cause of the nation's demise, but at 16:49f. also names this cause as social irresponsibility in a manner characteristic of the prophetic tradition as a whole. In summary, Ezekiel is to be interpreted, as indeed it interprets itself, in conjunction with the overall prophetic basis of judgment: oppression of the alien, poor, and powerless. This means, further, that the exegesis of Ezekiel cannot be correctly pursued on the premise of a narrow passageway to Leviticus 18:22 and 20:13 constructed on the unprovable assumption that Leviticus and Ezekiel imply the same thing by "abomination," once we move beyond the nonspecific meaning, "idolatry."

CULTIC PROSTITUTION IN THE OLD TESTAMENT

Examination of the references to cultic prostitution in the Old Testament yields results that are significantly akin to the uses of "abominations." The Hebrew root QDS, meaning holy or devoted, was applied to certain cultic functionaries, both female (*q^edesha*) and male (*qadesh*). In a discreetly reserved comment on 1 Kings 14:24, one of the six instances of the masculine form of this noun in the Hebrew Bible, John Gray says: "These persons were ministers of rites of imitative magic designed to promote fertility in nature. The administrative texts from Ras Shamra list such 'sacred persons' among the various classes and professions at Ugarit at the end of the Bronze Age, but do not specify their functions."[13]

Regarding the male *qadesh*, Boswell's statement that "there is no reason to assume that such prostitutes serviced persons of their own sex"[14] must be weighed carefully. In line with this, D.S. Bailey's opposition to the *King James* rendering of *qadesh* by "sodomite"[15] is certainly to be defended. The problem in translating *qadesh* is twofold: (1) the number of the occurrences of the word or its equivalent (in biblical or extrabiblical literature) is small and (2) even if one conjectures from the modest information available that the *qadesh*,

---

[13]John Gray, *I and II Kings*, 2d ed., Old Testament Library (Philadelphia: Westminster Press, 1970), p. 343. The Bronze Age ends at 1200 B.C.

[14]John Boswell, *Christianity, Social Tolerance, and Homosexuality* (Chicago: University of Chicago Press, 1980), p. 99.

[15]D.S. Bailey, *Homosexuality and the Western Christian Tradition* (London: Longmans, Green, 1955), p. 53.

like the q^edesha, served a sexual function, it is difficult to ascertain that this function was homosexual rather than heterosexual. To give this claim more substance it is necessary to take a sample of evidence provided by a well-accredited author, S.R. Driver, writing on Deuteronomy in the International Critical Commentary.

Already in 1902, Driver rejected the rendering of q^edesha and qadesh by "harlot" and "sodomite" in favor of "temple prostitute,"[16] so that the religious import of the term would be preserved in the translation. The Revised Standard Version's (RSV's) use of "cult prostitute" is in accord with this emphasis. In his discussion of female and male temple prostitution Driver cited the following sources: Herodotus 1.199; the Letter of Jeremiah 43; Strabo 12.36; Ramsay, Cities and Bishoprics of Phrygia 1.94f., 115; Lucian, Lucius, sec. 38; Athanasius, Contra Gentes 24E; Gesenius, Thesaurus s.v. Examination of these materials yields, however, far less than the reader might expect.

Herodotus History 1.199 refers only to female cult prostitutes. The same is true of the apocryphal Letter of Jeremiah 43 and Strabo Geography 12.3.36.[17] William M. Ramsay's remarks in The Cities and Bishoprics of Phrygia[18] are based on Strabo Geography 11.14.16, in which mention is made of male and female slaves dedicated to the goddess Anaitis, but the ensuing discussion concerns the females alone, and information on the function of the males is wholly lacking. Lucian (c. A.D. 120–180) in Lucius or the Ass tells a fable about Lucius becoming a donkey by use of a magic ointment,

[16]S.R. Driver, A Critical and Exegetical Commentary on Deuteronomy, 3d ed., International Critical Commentary (Edinburgh: T & T Clark, 1902), p. 265.

[17]Hans Conzelmann, "Korinth und die Mädchen der Aphrodite," Nachrichten der Wissenschaften in Göttingen 8 (1967–68):247–61, especially 259–61, and 1 Corinthians, trans. James W. Leitch, ed. George M. MacRae, Hermeneia (Philadelphia: Fortress Press, 1975), p. 12, n. 97, has evaluated Strabo's remarks (Geography 12.3.36; 11.14.16; and other pertinent passages). Conzelmann is concerned about claims, often based on Strabo, that the Corinthian temple of Aphrodite in Paul's day was a center of (female) sacred prostitutes numbering "more than a thousand." Conzelmann concludes from his study that Strabo's claim was valid neither for ancient Corinth (to which his famous remark refers) nor for the Roman period of Corinth (reestablished by Julius Caesar in 43 B.C., after incineration by the Romans a century before). Unfortunately, Conzelmann is much more critical in his reading of Strabo on temple prostitution, and even Herodotus, than he is of biblical texts like Deuteronomy 23:18f. and 2 Kings 23:7.

[18](Oxford: Clarendon Press, 1895), 1:94. P. 115 contains an inscription referring to a female cult prostitute.

while retaining his human senses and memory. True, the fable ridicules the catamite[19] habits of Philebus, who purchases the ass, and of his co-workers, who are servants of the Syrian goddess Atargatis. The work is obviously satirical. Does it contain dependable evidence on the conduct of male ministers of Atargatis? Without other corroboration one would have to say, doubtful. Athanasius (d. A.D. 373) discusses Phoenician female cult prostitutes and their male counterparts who "deny their own nature" and "assume a female nature"[20] in *Contra Gentes* 26. These comments are, however, plainly dependent on Romans 1:26f. and serve an apologetic aim. If Athanasius has information apart from Romans 1:26f., his reference could be cited as a late confirmation of a masculine, homosexual cultic prostitution. In Chapter Four, however, I argue that the moral-condemnatory use of Romans 1:26f. taken up by Athanasius in line with Wisdom 14:12–21 (cf. *Contra Gentes* sections 9 and 11) abandons the prophetic-liberationist viewpoint necessary for the correct exegesis of Romans 1:18–32.

The last reference from Driver is Gesenius' Latin *Thesaurus* under the word *qadesh*. It is not clear which edition of this *Thesaurus* Driver is using. (There are nine editions listed in volume 197 of the National *Union Catalogue Pre-1956 Imprints.*) In the 1905 fourteenth edition of Gesenius' *Handwörterbuch,*[21] however, Gesenius renders *qadesh* as a "'male prostitute,' 'catamite,' properly, 'one consecrated,' (approximately 'hierodoulos'[22])." But the 1907 English edition of Gesenius' *Lexicon*[23] abandons the translation "catamite," a change I regard as necessary on the same ground that Gunkel's introduction of pederasty into Genesis 19 has been criticized. This scanning of the evidence cited in Driver on male cultic prostitution shows it far less than convincing as a guide to homosexual acts in cultic rites.

[19]Greek *kinaidos* (Latin *cinaedus*) is usually rendered by English "catamite," defined in *Webster's Ninth New Collegiate* (p. 214) as "a boy kept by a pederast." In Lucian's tale it is not the kept but the keepers who are called *kinaidoi,* however.
[20]Athanasius, *Contra Gentes and De Incarnatione,* ed. and trans. Robert W. Thompson (Oxford: Clarendon Press, 1971), p. 69. Not knowing the edition of Athanasius used by Driver, I assume that he refers to section 26.
[21]Wilhelm Gesenius, *Handwörterbuch über das Alte Testament,* 14. Aufl., hrsg. v. H. Zimmern und F. Buhl (Leipzig: F.C.W. Vogel, 1905), p. 642.
[22]Greek *hierodoulos* means literally "temple slave" and is used by Strabo (e.g., *Geography* 11.4.7) to refer to both male and female temple functionaries.
[23]W. Gesenius, *Hebrew and English Lexicon of the Old Testament,* ed. F. Brown, S.R. Driver, and C.A. Briggs (Oxford: Clarendon Press, 1907), p. 873.

Hans-Joachim Schoeps has raised the intelligent question whether the rite of "holy marriage" (in the Canaanite agricultural cult) may have sprung from a prehistoric matriarchy.[24] If one posits, however, an early Canaanite matriarchy[25] as the ethos within which cultic prostitution as a biblical phenomenon emerged, the task is then shifted to the explaining of the role of the female rather than the male cultic functionary. This line of inquiry leads us afield from the specific texts and times our investigation obliges us to consider.

THE MALE CULT PROSTITUTE IN THE OLD TESTAMENT

The six occurrences of the masculine noun for cult prostitute (*qadesh*) in the Hebrew Bible are these: Deuteronomy 23:17 (Hebrew, vs. 18); 1 Kings 14:24; 15:12; 22:46; 2 Kings 23:7; and Job 36:14. It must be reemphasized that none of the prophets or their redactors use this word. Except for Job 36:14, one sees that all the occurrences of *qadesh* are located in the unit of Old Testament literature (Former Prophets plus Deuteronomy) attributed, as previously noted, to the editor-compiler called the Deuteronomic historian.[26]

In the absence of confirmatory, extrabiblical evidence on what functions the *qadesh* performed, it is understandable, if not provable, that John Boswell should hold that the sexual rites of the *qadesh* were with female rather than male devotees. More cautiously, Byron Shafer[27] concedes only that the *q^edeshim might* have

[24] Hans-Joachim Schoeps, "Überlegungen zum Problem der Homosexualität," *Der homosexuelle Nächste*, hrsg. v. Hermanus Bianchi u. a. (Hamburg: Furche, 1963), p. 91.

[25] Erich Fromm, *The Anatomy of Human Destructiveness* (New York: Holt, Rinehart & Winston, 1973), pp. 208–20, has discussed the "matricentric" society and religion of Çatal Hüyük, a seventh millennium B.C. town of Asia Minor. The archeological information is mainly taken from J. Mellaart, *Çatal Hüyük: A Neolithic Town in Anatolia* (New York: McGraw-Hill, 1967). The Baal-Astarte cult is obviously millennia subsequent to Çatal Hüyük and decidedly androcentric. Fromm's interest in the nonviolence of Çatal Hüyük leads to the further question of whether the Bronze Age patriarchy of Baal-Astarte does not represent the final absorption of matriarchy within phallic aggression.

[26] Cf. Bernard W. Anderson, *Understanding the Old Testament*, 3d ed. (Englewood Cliffs, NJ: Prentice-Hall, 1975), pp. 110f. The primary work goes back to Martin Noth, *Überlieferungsgeschichtliche Studien*, vol. 1 (Halle: Niemeyer, 1943).

[27] Byron E. Shafer, "The Church and Homosexuality," in *Minutes of the General Assembly of the United Presbyterian Church in the USA*, Part 1, Journal (New York: Office of the General Assembly of the United Presbyterian Church in the USA, November 1978), pp. 222–23. Shafer cautions that neither Hebrew nor Ugaritic texts disclose what the *qadesh* actually did. By letter (March 11, 1983) he grants that the office might have involved the heterosexual obligation.

served a heterosexual function. The reasons, however, for sustaining the view that same-sex rites belonged to the office of the *qadesh* can be stated as follows, even though the case for it cannot be said to be closed.

First, the context of the two prohibitions in Leviticus 18:22 and 20:13 suggests that what is opposed is not same-sex activity outside the cult, as in the modern secular sense, but within the cult identified as Canaanite.

Second, under patriarchy, only male members of the congregation were participants in ritual proceedings. Exodus 23:17 and 34:23 and Deuteronomy 16:16 prescribe, for example, that all the males of Israel are to appear before the Lord (at Passover, Pentecost, and Tabernacles). The story of Pharaoh's offer in Exodus 10:7–11 to let the male Israelites go serve their God rests on the same premise. It is not convincing, therefore, to assume that the *qadesh*, if sexual functions are assumed, should serve female worshipers.

Third, it is not a weighty objection that homosexual copulation can possess no meaning in a cult of reproductive fertility, because intercourse with the cult prostitute as representative of the deity was supposed to effect, in a magical way, the divine cosmic mystery of fructification, even among crops and animals. The cultic act transcended the biological union of the parties engaged in the ritual event.[28]

Fourth, the conjunction of male *qadesh* and female *q^edesha* in a text like Deuteronomy 23:17 (in which the sexual function of the female is not contested) does have modest evidential value in company with the arguments already mentioned.

If one assumes, however, that a large importance attaches to the view that the male cult prostitute did engage in homosexual acts, the conclusion presumes an emphasis inappropriate to the marked scarcity of evidence at one's command. A more significant line of inquiry presents itself in the preponderance of references to the female ministrants and in the comprehensive question why cultic prostitution, male or female, should come under Deuteronomic stricture. Does the moral ire represented in this stricture possess a

---

[28]Oskar Rühle, "Prostitution: I. Heilige Prostitution," *Die Religion in Geschichte und Gegenwart*, 2. Aufl., IV:1576–77. Beatrice A. Brooks, "Fertility Cult Functionaries in the Old Testament," *Journal of Biblical Literature* 60 (1941):243. Friedrich Heiler, *Die Frau in den Religionen der Menschheit* (New York: Walter de Gruyter, 1977), p. 28.

deeper and more enduring validity inaudible in the clamor of moralistic denunciations to which it has given rise?

In this regard the most fruitful suggestions arise from Gottwald's discussion of Rahab, the harlot of Jericho (Joshua 2; 6:15–27); the social setting of prostitution in ancient cities; and the rejection of sexual commodity fetishism in the religion of Jahweh.[29] The features accented in Gottwald's study have to do with Rahab's collaboration in the conquest of Jericho, a collaboration encouraged by her social position. Then, as now, commercial sex existed on the fringes of community life, officially disapproved (and therefore marginalized) but tolerated and exploited for its economic benefits. As hostess of spies (Joshua 2), Rahab does not identify with the power structure of Jericho. Her collaboration with the spies is aimed at the deliverance of her extended family (Joshua 2:12f.) when Jericho falls to the Hebrew conquest. Perhaps the family had given over Rahab to prostitution as a means of its own survival. If so, the strategy proved successful (Joshua 6:25).

The enlistment of prostitutes in the service of religion must be weighed from two considerations of economic power: (1) the gain to the temple system itself deriving from such prostitutes and (2) the gain to political power accruing from temple hierarchies who provide religious sanctions for royal politics. The biblical evidence for (1) is found in Deuteronomy 23:17f. and implied in all references to cultic prostitution, unless one makes the dubious assumption that cult prostitutes were themselves the sole recipients of the proceeds deriving from their sexual services. As to (2), the depth and power of prophecy in Israel emerges with marked frequency in its refusal to place on kingly power the approval of the cult. The refusal of this patronage from Elijah to Jeremiah and beyond is so intense and conspicuous in the emerging of Jewish apocalyptic as to make it central to the whole substance of prophetic religion.

For this discussion it is enough to point out that the "book of the law" (2 Kings 22:8), discovered in the eighteenth year of the Judean King Josiah (621 B.C.), is widely considered to be an early edition of Deuteronomy 12—26. Working with older sources, the Deuteronomic historian shapes a comprehensive story of the conquest of Canaan, the rise of monarchy, secession of the northern tribes after the reign of Solomon, the decline and fall of Samaria in

[29]Norman K. Gottwald, *The Tribes of Yahweh: A Sociology of the Religion of Liberated Israel, 1250–1050 B.C.* (Maryknoll, NY: Orbis Books, 1979), pp. 556–58, 694–96.

721 B.C. after the Assyrian deportation of King Hoshea, the southern struggle with Baalism, culminating in the Josianic reform. This narrative is consolidated around distinctive theological motifs of Deuteronomy: As a guarantee of successful conquest and perpetual tenure of the land, there is required a total faithfulness to the precepts of the Deuteronomic code, coupled with ruthless extermination of heathen shrines. Just as Baalistic corruption of the domain of Israel under Jeroboam (1 Kings 12:25–33) sealed its fate for destruction under the anger of God, the reform of Josiah, reconstituting the centrality and purity of the Jerusalem sanctuary, portended divine favor and national well-being. David Freedman sees the editor of the Deuteronomic history providing "simple answers to two great questions":

> Why did Samaria fall? and why is Josiah carrying out these alarming reforms? The answer to the first is, because of the sin of Jeroboam (1 Kings 13:34); the answer to the second is, because he is the long-awaited scion of the house of David and seeks to return to its ideals. That is, Josiah is taking drastic measures to eliminate apostasies which led to the fall of Samaria and which, according to the prophets, threaten the survival of Judah and Jerusalem.[30]

Although it is a widespread view that the Deuteronomic history resorts to the theology of the prophets in assessing the monarchs of Judah and Israel, this generalization should not eclipse the differences that exist between the Deuteronomic and prophetic standpoints. Acknowledging the Jahwistic strains of the Deuteronomist, Georg Fohrer does not hesitate to say that "it was not the Jahwism of Moses or of the great individual prophets, but the religion that developed in the course of the monarchy, with cultic and nationalistic emphasis and enriched through the addition of much that was originally Canaanite."[31] Robert Dobbie examined the prophetic and Deuteronomic attitudes to cultic sacrifice and effectively argued that the distinctiveness of the prophetic attitude in this regard was seriously compromised by an undiscriminating generalization blending the two traditions as one.[32]

The fact that five of the six uses of *qadesh* (sacred male prostitute)

[30] David N. Freedman, "Deuteronomic History, The," *Interpreter's Dictionary of the Bible Supplement,* ed. Keith Crim and others (Nashville: Abingdon Press, 1976), p. 227.

[31] Georg Fohrer, *History of Israelite Religion,* trans. David E. Green (Nashville: Abingdon Press, 1973), p. 300.

[32] Robert Dobbie, "Deuteronomy and the Prophetic Attitude to Sacrifice," *Scottish Journal of Theology* 12 (1959):68–82.

occur in Deuteronomic abnegations of idolatrous pollution, directly contributing to the nation's eventual demise through God's punitive judgment, is of importance when juxtaposed with the absence of the word among the prophets. Hosea was a contemporary of Jeroboam II (Hosea 1:1) and polemicizes, like the Deuteronomist, the high places (4:13; 8:4–13; 10:5–8; 12:11; 13:1f.). Hosea 4:14 refers to female sacral prostitution *(q^edesha)* but makes no corresponding attack on the male equivalent.

The first of the narrative texts, 1 Kings 14:24, for which Deuteronomy 23:17 serves as a summary legislative prohibition, links male temple prostitution and "abominations" in a manner already observed at Leviticus 18:22 and 20:13. The two following texts (1 Kings 15:12 and 22:46) speak redundantly of apparently futile efforts to eradicate the *q^edeshim.* The series climaxes in the purge of Josiah (2 Kings 23:7). It is noteworthy that all four narrative references pertain to the Jerusalem, rather than the Samaritan, setting: Rehoboam (1 Kings 14:24), Asa (1 Kings 15:12), Jehoshaphat (1 Kings 22:46), Josiah (2 Kings 23:7). In this fashion the reform of Josiah is climactic; he succeeds where predecessors fail. One must also consider whether the confinement of *q^edeshim* allusions to Jerusalem suggests a sacerdotal frame of reference for the movement to eradicate them. That is, the Holiness Code within which Leviticus 18:22 and 20:13 occur has an obvious sociological basis in the male priestly community. The language of 1 Kings 14:24 reminds one of the Leviticus parallels and is found in a literature for which the sole preeminence of the Jerusalem sanctuary is a major concern.[33] This is not an effort to say that male same-sex prostitution of a noncultic sort would *not* have produced texts like Deuteronomy 23:17[34] or Leviticus 18:22. It is, however, to suggest that the sacral

[33] Cf. Anderson, *Understanding the Old Testament*, p. 351. He affirms that Deuteronomy 18:1–18 prescribes that "country priests, who would lose their jobs with the closing of the local sanctuaries, are entitled to minister in the central sanctuary, although the writer in II Kings, who evidently knew that it was impractical for all these priests to join the Jerusalem staff, states that they found their livelihood by sojourning in the midst of their own people (II Kings 23:9)."

[34] In Deuteronomy 23:17–18 there is a parallel between *qadesh* and "dog" *(kelebh)*. Various commentators use the reference to underline the animal, immoral aspect of *qadesh* sexuality, but D. Winton Thomas, "*KELEBH* 'Dog': Its Origin and Some Usages of It in the Old Testament," *Vetus Testamentum* 10 (1960):423–26, finds the Akkadian *kalbu* (dog) in the Amarna letters used in the good sense of a faithful (civil) servant; its nonderogatory sense is also attested of cultic ministrants at shrines of Astarte in ancient Cyprus.

setting of the *qadesh* may be the specific aspect of it that prompted the reaction of the Deuteronomic historian.

One must not underestimate the moral consequences resulting from the rendering of *qadesh* as "sodomite" in the *King James Version* at those passages I have discussed in the Deuteronomic history. Peter Coleman seeks to defend the translation on the ground that in the English of Thomas Cranmer (sixteenth-century shaper of Protestant churchly language), "sodomy" referred to sexual vice in general rather than to the specific modern sense of anal intercourse.[35]

This is unsatisfactory. The *King James* "sodomite" welded together in a total moral-theological amalgam an exegesis of Genesis 19, declaring a divine wrathful judgment-unto-destruction provoked by attempted same-sex intercourse on the one hand, with the institution of male cultic prostitution in the Deuteronomic compilation on the other hand. This is an ideological construction justified, so it is said, on the basis of a long-forgotten connotation of the word sodomites in the vocabulary of Thomas Cranmer. The *English Revised Version* of 1885, Cranmer notwithstanding, perpetuated in these passages the use of "sodomites." That the RSV forsook "sodomites" for "cult prostitutes" is a significant improvement in terms of its moral potentiality for dealing with oppression of homosexuals in the religious community. It must be recognized, however, that the *Authorized Version* of 1611 enjoyed a language power and thereby a social influence that no single modern version can expect to enjoy. Indeed, in the evangelical-conservative community, in which homophobic attitudes tend to predominate, receptiveness to the RSV was, at best, unfavorable. The *Authorized Version* enjoyed continuing widespread use, and a plethora of additional versions obviating the RSV kept appearing.

A final, monumental difficulty of the Deuteronomic history must now be named: After the fall and exile of Judah (587 B.C.), it "becomes essentially untenable."[36] That is, the reform of Josiah, designed to restore conditions of obedience that are to guarantee (cf. Deuteronomy 30:15–20) perpetual tenure of the land, proves itself

[35] Coleman, *Christian Attitudes*, p. 43. Bailey's attempt (*Homosexuality*, p. 53) to root out the translation "sodomites" is to be commended, even if it is not possible to concede without reservation that *q^edeshim* does not imply male homosexual intercourse. For current definition of sodomy, see n. 1 of this chapter.

[36] Freedman, "Deuteronomic History," p. 227.

incapable of delivering on this guarantee. Consequently, David Freedman sees in 2 Kings 23:26 ("Still the Lord did not turn from the fierceness of his great wrath, by which his anger was kindled against Judah, because of all the provocations with which Manasseh had provoked him") a "forced attempt to explain why Josiah failed."[37] On the basis of this analysis of the net result of the Deuteronomic history, let us grant for the moment the full claim of a Justinian understanding of the rise and fall of civilizations, specifically that toleration of homosexual behavior could only eventuate in an anger of God so intense that the destruction of the city (nation, civilization) would surely follow. But 2 Kings 23 proves the belief untenable. Sodom's "sin" is eradicated under Josiah, but the axe still falls because of an anger of God retroactive to the "abominations" of Manasseh (2 Kings 21:1–18)!

Marvin Pope translated Job 36:14 (the last of the passages using *qadesh*) by returning to the *King James* use of "sodomites":

> Their soul dies in youth,
> Their life among the sodomites.[38]

He comments: "The usual explanation is that the orgiastic excesses imposed on the hierodules so debilitated them that their predisposition to early mortality became proverbial." As to the life span of the *qᵉdeshim*, in the absence of any statistical evidence apropos to the subject, one would tend to regard "the usual explanation" as firmly based on conjecture and expressive of a homophobic viewpoint. This does not remove the fact that Elihu, who voices the proverb of 36:14, scorns the male cult prostitutes as he does the godless

[37] Ibid.
[38] Marvin Pope, *Job*, 3d ed., The Anchor Bible (New York: Doubleday, 1973), p. 267. In Job 31:31 ("If males of my household ever said, 'O that we might sate ourselves with his flesh'"), Pope finds Job affirming that his men were not allowed to abuse strangers homosexually (ibid., p. 236). He holds that "flesh" (Hebrew *basar*) in this verse means "phallus," as in Ezekiel 16:26 and 23:20, and certainly so in Leviticus 15:2–15, which deals with *gonorrhea benigna.* On these grounds one might see in Job 31:31–32 another indirect reference to Genesis 19, and the passage could be listed with those texts discussed in n. 9 of this chapter.

The major objection to taking "flesh" as "phallus" in verse 31 would be that the phraseology seems only to refer to the insertee and thus is not applicable to the phallic aggression the text is said to disavow. The translation of Job 31:31 is at best uncertain; cf. *The New English Bible:* "Have the men of my household never said, 'Let none of us speak ill of him!'" In favor of Pope's emphasis, however, Job 31:32 does echo Genesis 19:2f. and Judges 19:15, 20.

(36:13). Job, in general, does not place much credence, however, in the wisdom of his counselors, and there is no convincing reason for us to do otherwise.

TRADITIONS IN CONFLICT—A LIBERATIONIST SOLUTION

It is now possible to draw together the threads of the foregoing sections and propose a solution to the problem presented by them. Despite abundant opportunity to do so, no prophet adduces sodomy as the cause of the nation's fall. No prophet uses the noun for male cult prostitute or discusses the activity such a person pursued. The prophets, in fact, are as silent on the subject of homosexual acts as is the whole tradition of the New Testament teaching of Jesus. This is a significant silence.[39]

Over against the silence of the prophetic books exists a collection of texts (Leviticus 18:22; 20:13; Deuteronomy 23:17f.; 1 Kings 14:24; 15:12; 22:46; 2 Kings 23:7; and Job 36:14) in which male cultic prostitution, which possibly involved homosexual acts, is implicitly disapproved or explicitly prohibited. In all these passages—except the two from Leviticus—the noun for male cult prostitute is found. So it is probable that with the two Leviticus texts male cultic prostitution is also intended. The reason for this follows.

Contextually, Leviticus 18:22 ("You shall not lie with a male as with a woman; it is an abomination") stands between a prohibition of child sacrifice to the Ammonite deity, Molech (cf. 1 Kings 11:7), and the rule against bestiality in 18:23. Carl Keil traced the latter to the Egyptian ram cult.[40] Thus on both sides 18:22 is enclosed by jabs at foreign cult practice. S.R. Driver links Leviticus 18:22 therefore to his discussion of the precept against cultic prostitution in Deuteronomy 23:17f., concluding that "Leviticus 18:22 (cf. 20:13), though general in its wording is aimed probably at the same prac-

---

[39]This silence does not mean that homosexuality did not exist throughout the history of Israel and down through New Testament times. Indeed, our assumption is the opposite. Homosexuality has existed in all civilizations at all periods, whether overtly or covertly. It is a natural form of sexual expression of a minority of persons, both male and female. The major problem of the homosexual community has not been, as a rule, its own sexuality but the intolerance it has encountered in the sexual majority.

[40]Carl F. Keil, *Biblischer Commentar über die Bücher Mose's*, 2. Bd. *Leviticus, Numbri und Deuteronomium* (Leipzig: Dörffling und Franke, 1862), p. 119.

tise."[41] In addressing Leviticus 18:22 Norman Snaith does not hesitate to say: "Thus homosexuality here is condemned on account of its association with idolatry."[42]

Chapters 17—26 of Leviticus have been designated the Holiness Code since the work of August Klostermann in 1877. The Code's preoccupation is purity of worship. The theme is expressed repeatedly: "You shall be holy; for I the Lord your God am holy [19:2; cf. 18:21; 19:30; 20:7, 26, etc.]."

Paul Humbert has, furthermore, observed that "abomination" (to^{c}eba) occurs six times in the Holiness Code and nowhere else in Leviticus or in the priestly stratum of the Pentateuch.[43] All six of these occurrences are confined to Leviticus 18 and 20 and are further restricted to the context of sex impurity, four of them in chapter 18 (vss. 26–27, 29–30) in proximity to the first instance in 18:22. The single remaining instance is found at Leviticus 20:13! On the basis of what we have observed previously about the meaning of to^{c}eboth as referring to idolatry in Ezekiel, it is understandable that Snaith comments on the use of "abomination" in 18:22: "Usually this word to^{c}ebah has to do with idolatrous actions, actions connected with the cult of other gods."[44]

Because there is increasing awareness that male sacral prostitution—the absence of reference to homosexual acts among women in the sex laws of the Holiness Code illustrates the patriarchal perspective—is morally irrelevant to private, consensual, nonsacral homosexuality, other nonsacral grounds are frequently sought. Primary among these is the appeal to "natural law," especially since it can be shown that the New Testament adapted from Greek moral

[41] Driver, *Deuteronomy*, p. 264. Likewise, Von Rad, *Genesis*, p. 217.

[42] Norman Snaith, ed., *Leviticus and Numbers*, The Century Bible (Nashville: Thomas Nelson, 1967), p. 126.

[43] Paul Humbert, "Le substantiv to^{c}ēbā et le verbe t^{c}b dans l'Ancien Testament," *Zeitschrift für die alttestamentliche Wissenschaft* 72 (1960):232.

[44] Snaith, *Leviticus and Numbers*, p. 126. Numerous other features of Levitical holiness more or less incomprehensible to modern secularity may be explainable on this same ground: association with idol worship. For example, Schoeps, *Der homosexuelle Nächste*, p. 89, points out that the wild pig, according to the Ras Shamra texts, was holy to the Alijan Baal; hence its proscription in Leviticus 11:7f. and Deuteronomy 14:8. The Jahwist (Genesis 43:32) discloses that table fellowship with Hebrews was an abomination to the Egyptians, as also the shepherd (Genesis 46:36). This probably reflects a priestly, cultic (Exodus 8:26), and xenophobic "purity" on the Egyptian side that was the obverse of the Hebrew one.

philosophy various admonitions based on appeals to "nature." Peter Coleman pursues this line of argument with considerable subtlety.[45]

Discussing the law against sexual intercourse with animals (Leviticus 18:23 and 20:15–16; cf. Exodus 22:19 and Deuteronomy 27:21) that occurs in context with the proscription of homosexual acts in both Leviticus 18 and 20, Coleman affirms that "the concept of what is abomination to God takes on a further meaning, in which it has some embryonic sense of natural law." Despite his refusal to read into this "embryonic" natural law stoic ideas of "the framework of the universe" as were later absorbed into Christian scholasticism, Coleman still succeeds in shifting the Levitical foundation toward modern rationalism. This is particularly evident when he climaxes his résumé of reasons for the law against homosexuality as follows: "The consensus of the Semitic peoples against homosexuality coalesced with ordinary homophobia and was then strengthened and perhaps transmuted by a doctrine of creation and sexuality that came to understand human sexual nature as intended to find its physical expression only within certain recognized limits."[46]

The objection to this modernization of Leviticus must be bluntly stated. It is unconvincing not only because it is unresponsive to contemporary scientific perspectives on homosexuality (emphasized in Chapter One), but also because it reduces to the vanishing point the uniquely masculine and hieratic quality of the Holiness Code and inadequately questions the use of natural law as an instrument of human oppression. The determination of what is "natural" deserves as much ideological suspicion as any other time-honored power structure, having been claimed as the basis for the divine right of kings, all-male priesthoods, and androcentric matrimonial customs. The fact that the New Testament borrows from stoic rationalism moral injunctions based on what is perceived as the cosmic structure of reality increases rather than diminishes the appropriateness of liberationist thought and sociological criticism. The natural/unnatural discussion of homosexuality readily translates into the fruitless sloganeering decried in the clinical experience of Masters and Johnson: "My way is better than your way." The inability of discussions based on this premise to advance moral insights has been sensibly analyzed by Kenneth Dover:

[45] Coleman, *Christian Attitudes*, pp. 49–51.
[46] Ibid., p. 51.

A surprising amount of thought and feeling has been devoted in our time to the question whether homosexual relations are "unnatural," and, if so, in what sense. Since I observe that any community encourages behaviour which it regards as probably conducive to an eventual situation of a kind desired by that community and discourages behaviour which seems likely to hinder the development of such a situation, and since the absence of any clear correlation between "nature" and desirability seems to me self-evident, I cannot engage with any enthusiasm in debates about the naturalness or unnaturalness of homosexuality.[47]

In Jacob Neusner's work *The Idea of Purity in Ancient Judaism*[48] there is an interesting exchange with anthropologist Mary Douglas. These writers differ at a fundamental point, namely, whether purity rules of the sort found in Leviticus serve as instruments of social coercion. In this exchange, one must agree with Douglas that "not to see how they arise as part of the social process is tantamount to supposing that they emerge mysteriously fully fledged and independent of the communities in which they are respected."[49]

Neusner uses in connection with these purity rules the expression "priestly propaganda"[50] in voicing his doubt that such rules represented the larger world of Israelite conceptions; but Douglas responds that the very phrase "priestly propaganda" implies the desire to influence or coerce, regardless of how effective such attempts might have been. She cites in this connection the anathemas against foreign cults and foreign wives and validates her argument from laws on women's uncleanness and sexuality: "As to the manifold rules which attribute impurity to women, in menses or childbirth, ask the Women's Liberation Movement about the intention to sustain male dominance. And to declare all improper sex impure, is not that a blow struck in defence of marriage and family?"[51]

Thus far I have attempted to establish two bodies of evidence in Old Testament tradition. In the prophetic books, on the one hand, I have found no polemic against male homosexual acts either within or apart from temple prostitution, and I have established that the Sodom tradition of frightful judgment is not linked to same-sex

[47] Kenneth J. Dover, *Greek Homosexuality* (Cambridge, MA: Harvard University Press, 1978), p. 154, n. 1.
[48] (Leiden: E.J. Brill, 1973), pp. 119–30, 139–42.
[49] Ibid., pp. 140–41.
[50] Ibid., pp. 120–21.
[51] Ibid., p. 141.

intercourse. There exists, on the other hand, within the Holiness Code and Deuteronomic history[52] a tradition that, by statute or implication, condemns male cultic homosexuality.

These two traditions, substantially at variance in character, have been in Judeo-Christian interpretation pasted together as one establishmentarian and homophobic amalgam, precious to the perpetuation of biblical pietism while placing in eclipse the moral depth and liberative power of prophetic faith. The amalgamation of these traditions and the consequent censoring of the most distinctive features within them has been brought about by an exegetical tour de force consisting at minimum of the following:

- the identification of the rapists of Genesis 19 with the institution of sacral prostitution and vice versa
- the creation of a special language (sodomy, sodomite) that encourages a unilinear view[53] of Sodom essentially heretical in its impact
- the assumption that when "high places" or female cult prostitution is mentioned, male homosexual acts are also implied and condemned
- the indiscriminate modernization of references to cult prostitution by making them applicable to noncultic homosexuality
- a false form of historical interpretation that shields the interpreter from the qualifying impact of new knowledge also disclosing God's truth.

One of the distinctive features of medieval exegesis was the rule of analogy.[54] First used as a criterion of biblical interpretation by

[52] Once again, these texts are Leviticus 18:22; 20:13; Deuteronomy 23:17; 1 Kings 14:24; 15:12; 22:46; 2 Kings 23:7. Job 36:14 may be included in this tradition but belongs of course to Wisdom literature, rather than to the Holiness Code or Deuteronomic history. Yet one must recall that Job, although sapiential, is also liberationist, as Ernst Bloch pungently maintained.

[53] The "one-line" view of Genesis 19 not only missed the point of the overarching hospitality theme that Gunkel and others found in the saga but also distorted phallic aggression into something other than the grasping, imperialistic machismo the story exposes. Heresy (Greek *haireō*, "grasp" or "seize") means to seize on and ride into the ground a fragment of a larger, manifold truth. Thus the one-line view of Genesis 19 in biblical pietism is fundamentally heretical.

[54] The phrase "analogy of faith" derives from Romans 12:6 *(kata tēn analogian tēs pisteōs)* and means "according to the proportion of faith" ("the faith" or "our faith" is also possible). In Thomas Aquinas the phrase signified explaining scripture in accord with scripture, hence "analogy of scripture." In application, however, analogy came to mean that no interpretation contrary to established belief was tolerable. In Protes-

Origen, analogy was always plagued with the dilemma of making the text fit the dogma or conforming the dogma to the text, especially when related texts did not speak with one accord. With the increase of biblical authority in the sixteenth century, the analogy of scripture became increasingly important, even if a considerable latitude of theological conceptions resulted within the single canon.

In the modern period, as a result of historical-critical exegesis, the impact of the Enlightenment, and the decline of authoritative "systems" of doctrine as lens through which scripture had to be comprehended, the diversity of biblical-theological possibilities has been richly increased. What L.E. Keck and G.M. Tucker have called "the tyranny of a homogeneous sacred book"[55] has been effectively broken, even if its banners still fly within sects not yet moved by the historical-critical method. Historical criticism, of course, yields its own tyranny and reduces scripture to a depository of interesting or uninteresting historical antiquities, if no liberationist commitments move the exegete.

It has been argued in this chapter that the system of homophobic beliefs erected from passages not inherently analogous, but only treated so as a result of ideological reasoning, should no longer be tolerated. It is salutary for the work of theology, the integrity of religion, and the state of human civilization that biblical culture can no longer coerce social existence. This is not because biblical culture has nothing redemptive to contribute, or because secular society does not invariably proceed with its own autonomous idol making, but because the cruciform character of Christian belief repudiates the establishmentarian role and its power of coercion, taking into serious account the hiddenness of the God who seeks out and blesses the poor and powerless, puts down the princes from their thrones, and exalts those of low degree.

---

tantism also the emerging of new orthodoxies to control the meaning of biblical texts is futile, if understandable from the standpoint of ecclesiastical power. Cf. Frederic W. Farrar, *History of Interpretation* (London: Macmillan, 1886), pp. 332–33.

[55] L.E. Keck and G.M. Tucker, "Exegesis," *Interpreter's Dictionary Supplement*, p. 303.

CHAPTER FOUR

The Theology of Gay/Lesbian Liberation in the New Testament

The study of New Testament teaching on homosexuality is usually concentrated on Romans 1:26–27; 1 Corinthians 6:9–10; and 1 Timothy 1:10. Sometimes Jude 7 is also introduced, together with its secondary parallel in 2 Peter 2:6–8, because of the mention of Sodom and Gomorrah.

The argument may be summarized briefly. First, the 1979 work of Victor Paul Furnish concerning homosexuality in Paul's moral teaching[1] is described as an intelligent exposition of important Pauline emphases within the canons of historical criticism. These insights are then criticized in the light of perspectives from gay/lesbian liberation theology. Finally, on the basis of Romans 1:26–27 the case is made that the understanding of Paul is correctly disclosed only when the liberationist perspective is used intentionally. The passages from 1 Timothy, Jude, and 2 Peter are discussed in a final postscript.

A CONTEMPORARY DISCUSSION OF HOMOSEXUALITY IN PAUL'S THEOLOGY

Professor Furnish, of the Perkins School of Theology (Southern Methodist University, Dallas, Texas), teaches within a Protestant heritage that gives to social and moral questions a position of distinct importance. His 1968 work, *Theology and Ethics in Paul*, had al-

[1]Victor Paul Furnish, *The Moral Teaching of Paul* (Nashville: Abingdon Press, 1979).

ready qualified him as a primary contributor to the study of Pauline ethics. This can be verified by examining in Ernst Käsemann's magisterial commentary on Romans[2] the number of corroborative references to Furnish.

The third chapter of his 1979 work, *The Moral Teaching of Paul,* contains Furnish's discussion of homosexuality. He objects to the noun sodomites found in the English versions, pointing out that "no Hebrew or Greek word formed on the name 'Sodom' ever appears in the biblical manuscripts on which these versions are based."[3] So he commends the *Revised Standard Version* (RSV) for abandoning the *King James* rendering of *qadesh* by "sodomite" in the Deuteronomic history and using the more accurate "male cult prostitute." (Since 1971, inexplicably, the RSV retains "sodomites" only at 1 Timothy 1:10.[4]) Furnish rightly emphasizes that the male cult prostitutes are attacked in the Old Testament not because they commit same-sex acts, but because they serve idol cults.

After a brief treatment of Greek pederasty in the works of Plato, Seneca, Plutarch, and Dio Chrysostom, in which predominantly negative reports on pederasty are emphasized, Furnish turns to the prohibitions of homosexual acts in the Holiness Code (Leviticus 18:22, 20:13) and Philo's discussion of Sodom in his work *On Abraham.* Three comments conclude this survey:

1. The moral writings, both biblical and extrabiblical, which inform Paul's judgments in the first century A.D., have no understanding of same-sex orientaton comparable to that provided in modern psychology and sociology.
2. Seneca, Dio Chrysostom, and Philo associate homosexual practice with insatiable lust and gross luxury.
3. By Paul's time moral philosophers had come to believe same-sex practice inevitably involved exploitation of one person by another and was a violation of the law of nature.[5]

---

[2] Ernst Käsemann, *Commentary on Romans,* trans. and ed. G.W. Bromiley (Grand Rapids, MI: Wm. B. Eerdmans, 1980). See, for example, pp. 113, 137, 138, 142, 172, 174, 175, 176, 179, 180, 183, 227, 324, 326, 330, 331.

[3] Furnish, *Moral Teaching of Paul,* pp. 57–58.

[4] Furnish correctly denies the Pauline authorship of 1 Timothy. The ethic of the Pastorals (1 and 2 Timothy, Titus) definitely tends toward a blunting of Paul's more radical insights. In this vein RSV translators may have retained "sodomites" at 1 Timothy 1:10 as a less than adequate imitation of Paul's way of thinking!

[5] Summarized from Furnish, ibid., pp. 65–67.

Furnish now turns to 1 Corinthians 6:9.[6] Previously, in 1 Corinthians 5, Paul deals with a case of incest (5:1–8) followed by a clarification of his previous admonition that the church should shun fornicators (5:9–13). This brings up disciplinary action, and Paul insists that judgments should be sought within the church, not by court proceedings before unbelievers (6:1–8). Unbelievers are "unrighteous" (6:9), not saints, as are believers (6:11).

The apostle's argument assumes that believers do not, in reality, belong to this world. Verses 6:9–10 spell out in more detail who the unrighteous are by using a list of evildoers (a form of moral instruction Judaism adapted from gentile moral philosophy). Some of the Corinthians were once like that but have now been justified and set apart through baptism (6:11). In the catalogue of wrongdoers at 6:9 the two Greek words *malakoi* and *arsenokoitai* were rendered in the first edition of the RSV by the one word homosexuals. This was changed in the 1971 revision to "sexual perverts." Furnish finds Paul's attitude in 1 Corinthians 6:9 conforming in general to the disapproval expressed in Philo, Dio Chrysostom, and Seneca.

Furnish proceeds next[7] to the more important passage, Romans 1:26–27: "Their women exchanged natural relations for unnatural, and the men likewise gave up natural relations with women and were consumed with passion for one another, men committing shameless acts with men and receiving in their own persons the due penalty for their error." Again, this disapproving statement expresses the same attitude found in Seneca, Philo, and others that same-sex acts arise from insatiable sexual lust and that such acts are "unnatural."

In the section Romans 1:18—3:20 the need of all (gentile and Jew) for the grace of God is underlined. Verses 1:18–32 denounce gentile unrighteousness along lines found in Hellenistic Judaism, especially the Book of Wisdom, which repudiates gentile religions as "foolish idolatries." God sends on the idolators (Wisdom 11—12) punishments suited to the deeds. This is like the statement (Romans 1:18) that "the wrath of God is revealed from heaven against all ungodliness and wickedness" or "the dishonorable passions" of Romans 1:26–27 to which God gives them up. Even a list of vices to match Romans 1:29–31 is found at Wisdom 14:25–26: "bloody murder,

[6] Ibid., pp. 68–73.
[7] Ibid., pp. 73–78.

72

theft and fraud, corruption, treachery, riot, perjury, honest men driven to distraction, ingratitude, moral corruption, sexual perversion,[8] breakdown of marriage, adultery, debauchery [NEB]." All these vices derive directly from idolatry (Wisdom 14:27).

The kinship of Paul's ideas in Romans 1:18–32, the Book of Wisdom, and traditional Jewish reasoning about gentile idolatry producing moral, especially sexual, depravity is clear. What Paul says about homosexual acts could have been written by Plutarch or Dio Chrysostom if abstracted from its setting in Romans 1:18–32.

After establishing thus Paul's condemnation of homosexual practices (a marginal concern found only in the two passages from Paul, 1 Corinthians 6:9 and Romans 1:26f.), Furnish turns to the contemporary application of these teachings.[9] His four emphases can be summarized:

1. Paul provides no answers to questions the modern church asks about homosexuals, such as whether they should be admitted to membership, permitted to assume offices, or be ordained to ministry. "It is mistaken to invoke Paul's name in support of any specific position on these matters."

2. Paul, like Hellenistic Judaism, counted homosexual practice a gentile vice, linked to pagan idolatry, a deliberate choice rooted in gross sexual appetite. These attitudes are, however, outmoded on the basis of current sexology. "It is also clear that homosexual behavior does not necessarily involve sexual exploitation of another person." The "unnatural" premise also collapses when, for example, in 1 Corinthians 11:14–15 Paul finds long hair unnatural for men. As a matter of fact, "the only 'natural' thing is to let one's hair grow as long as it will!"

3. "Paul's fundamental concerns about homosexual practice (as he understood it) are as valid in the twentieth century as they were in the first." But it is not possible to believe with Paul that homosexual conduct always involves "rebellion against the Creator and his creation, the debasement of one's own true identity and the exploitation of another's."

[8] This phrase *(enallage geneseos)* appears to represent in short form what is said in Romans 1:26–27.
[9] *Moral Teaching of Paul,* pp. 78–82.

4. In the total design of Romans 1:18–32 is a preface to Paul's indictment of the Jews—"they are no better"—and the assertion that all are in need of God's grace (2:1—3:20).

FURNISH'S CONTRIBUTION IN LIBERATIONIST PERSPECTIVE

At a number of important points Furnish's analysis confirms observations I have made previously. It is encouraging and hopeful that an established New Testament scholar is willing to enter an arena in which the contest is so heated and to advance positions that are unpopular in church and synagogue. He seeks to inform himself from modern medicine and psychology, recognizing that the evaluation of biblical ideas cannot disregard such information. His discussion of natural/unnatural sex reminds us of Kenneth Dover's warning that "natural" becomes a coded way for expressing what a community desires, and there is no demonstrated connection between nature and community desire. Dover has further emphasized that what is natural and normal may signify only what is customary in a given community: "Why the Greek of the classical period accepted homosexual desire as natural and normal is a much easier question: they did so because previous generations had accepted it, and segregation of the sexes in adolescence fortified and sustained the acceptance and the practise."[10]

From the liberationist perspective the appeal to what is "natural" often conceals the imposition on the community of customs that disregard the interests of some to the advantage of others. "What's good for General Motors" can indeed represent the economic well-being of a considerable community, including stockholders, directors, and workers. When Reinhold Niebuhr spoke of sin as "undue self regard," he did not intend that an unqualified altruism, if humanly possible, would eradicate evil. The evil arises when one's benefit is elevated into and confused with the benefit of the entire community. When the good of General Motors is confused with the good of the country, a definite element of narcissism and imperialism has driven self-regard out of its bounds. Even when custom is legalized by due process and imposed by majority vote, truth may be distorted and justice undone.

Paul recognized fully the dynamic and conflictual aspect of reli-

[10]Kenneth J. Dover, "Classical Attitudes to Sexual Behaviour," *Arethusa* 6 (1973):66.

gious and moral insight in 1 Corinthians 1:18–31 that speaks of God as choosing the things that are not *(ta mē onta)* to put to nought the things that are (vs. 28). This means that the perspective of Christian belief, both theological and moral, is always "meontic" (i.e., aimed not at what *is* but what, in God, has the potentiality for being). In this sense it is not only correct but also necessary in evaluating Paul's view of human sexuality to distinguish the legal from the liberative element and give precedence to the latter.

There is also a gender consideration for refusing to accept uncritical definitions of natural sexuality constructed by the heterosexual majority, by Stoic philosophers, or even by the apostle Paul. Furnish intelligently rebuts Paul's claim (1 Corinthians 11:14–15) that a man should have short hair, a woman, long hair. But liberationist thought carries this insight a stage further by closer attention to the androcentric setting in which the hair doctrine is located.

Disharmonious and conflicting perspectives on manhood and womanhood are found in 1 Corinthians 11. The head of every man is Christ, and the head of the woman is the man (vs. 3); the woman should be veiled (vss. 5–6), because the man is the image and glory of God, but the woman is the glory of man (vs. 7); woman derives from man (vs. 8); she was created for man (vs. 9) and ought to wear a veil as a sign of subordination (vs. 10). Verses 11 and 12 interrupt this by emphasizing male-female equality and mutuality, causing Hans Conzelmann to comment: "Here the proof that has so far been offered seems to be invalidated. For now both sexes appear to be equal after all. The transition with *plēn*, "of course," already marks a note of retreat. The contradiction between v 8 and v 12 seems particularly crass."[11]

It seems, therefore, impossible not to consider 1 Corinthians 11:14–15 as grounded in male dominance and female dependency. Although Conzelmann[12] and others have made good arguments that 1 Corinthians 14:33–36 (let women keep silence in the churches) is a non-Pauline interpolation, Werner Kümmel confidently affirms that there is no objective basis for counting the passage spurious,[13] and

[11]Hans Conzelmann, *1 Corinthians*, trans. James W. Leitch and ed. George M. MacRae, Hermeneia (Philadelphia: Fortress Press, 1975), p. 190. Conzelmann senses that 1 Corinthians 11:16 "shows that Paul does not completely trust any of his grounds [p. 191]."

[12]Ibid., p. 246.

[13]Werner G. Kümmel, *Introduction to the New Testament*, rev. ed., trans. Howard C. Kee (Nashville: Abingdon Press, 1975), pp. 275–76.

one wonders whether Conzelmann bases his view on moral grounds tipped toward the liberated Paul rather than the patriarchal Paul. It is certain that in the absence of significant and unexpected manuscript evidence, 1 Corinthians 14:33–36 will remain part of the canonical Corinthian corpus and will have to be opposed by morally discerning Christians.

In Galatians 3:28 Paul pronounces the end of distinctions between male and female. The eschatological reality is boldly defended. Viewing the unreconciled disparity between Paul's concept of human freedom through the gospel and his support of male dominance, Elisabeth Moltmann-Wendel sees the latter as a vestige of Paul's cultural captivity:

> Paul, who had such impressive female coworkers, and whose work would probably not have been possible without them, is an example of how difficult it is to forget an education shaped by men. He was absolutely convinced that in Christ there is no difference between man and woman. Galatians 3:28 is the decisive passage in which he made clear that the old Jewish separation between peoples, social groups, and men and women no longer existed in the new community. This was also a central point of the gospel for the learned rabbi. But when it came to questions of style and behavior, elements of patriarchal thought patterns on order kept oozing out of him—elements which had not yet been assimilated by his new insight.[14]

At the foundation of Paul's theology is faith righteousness or justification by faith. Over against this stands legal rectitude, which Paul sought and enjoyed before his awareness of the significance of Christ crucified (Philippians 3:6). Faith righteousness is that liberty before which legal rectitude is ultimately revealed as unmistakable bondage (Galatians 2:4; 5:1). In Galatians 2:11–21 Paul demonstrates the fundamental sociological meaning of faith justification as freedom. Peter's refusal to continue in table fellowship with gentiles (2:12) is such a breach of the freedom he ought to exercise and to which the gentile Christians of Antioch have also been called that it reduces to nil the cross of Christ (Galatians 2:21). In this instance Paul acts out basic cultural implications of the liberationist mandate of the gospel and spells them out in Galatians 3:28. If, furthermore, Peter's cultural captivity to ethnic chauvinism must be overcome on the same premise by which Paul's own androcentricity is correctly

[14]Elisabeth Moltmann-Wendel, *Liberty, Equality, Sisterhood*, trans. Ruth Gritsch (Philadelphia: Fortress Press, 1978), p. 27.

criticized,[15] the liberationist solution to the issue of homosexual exclusion is a necessary corollary of this same premise. The walls of separation must come down.

Furnish effectively nullifies the sexological assumptions used by Paul in regarding homosexual acts in themselves as unnatural or invariably exploitative. The ground is laid in this manner for an appeal to the theology of liberation so widely expressed in Paul as a positive basis for homosexual inclusion. One meets instead the declaration that it is "mistaken to invoke Paul's name in support of any specific position" on matters like homosexual membership in the mainline churches or homosexuals holding offices in these churches or being ordained as pastors. It would be a significant step forward indeed from where we now are if priests, ministers, and rabbis were to desist from the use of biblical texts for condemnation of homosexuals. In the absence, however, of an affirmative basis for inclusion and for overcoming the repressive and discriminatory treatment of homosexuals, church and synagogue usually stand apart from the struggle for gay/lesbian rights. One fears that the inability of Paul to speak either yea or nay to the difficult decisions that both homosexuals and heterosexuals must make can be traced back in large measure to the negative result of historical interpretation—the confinement of a text's meaning to the circumstances of its own time and place. A striking example of this is found in *New Testament Ethics* by Jack T. Sanders, which concludes in effect that the New Testament is so bound to its own time (e.g., the quality of New Testament eschatology) that it can speak no moral message across the chasm dividing the first and twentieth centuries.[16]

It is an enduring benefit of the evangelical-liberal tradition that it affirms and defends the historical-critical method of biblical inquiry, but the theology of liberation is, nevertheless, the appropriate modality for present biblical education because it sustains serious connection with the biblical roots of both Judaism and Christianity, because it calls for a comprehensive theological commitment that can cope with the void of scientific objectivity, because it provides intelligent correlation of cognitive and sociological categories of human existence, and because it offers biblical education its best road of exit from ethical vacuity and academic elitism.

[15] Acts 10:1—11:19 confirms this from the Lucan standpoint, even if Luke does not clearly discern Paul's radical attitude toward legal rectitude.

[16] (Philadelphia: Fortress Press, 1975).

The question of patriarchy in Paul is not irrelevant to his attitude toward homoerotic acts. On the basis of ideas drawn from Vanggaard and Dover, I have attempted earlier to establish the common ground of Genesis 19 and Judges 19 as a phallic aggression issuing in gang rape of either male or female. The distinct ingredient in phallic aggression is power over the victim, a power associated in patriarchy with masculinity as such. Its connection with both sexual violence and death is not atypical, as Mary Daly has correctly discerned in her discussion of rape, genocide, and war.[17] I would further argue that the eclipsing of phallic aggression in the exegesis of Genesis 19 and Judges 19—accomplished by the introduction of Canaanite cultic prostitution, or pederasty (at Sodom) or cosmetic improvements in the behavior of the Levite (at Gibeah)—serves the subtle purpose of shifting the horrific guilt in these stories from the account of masculinity run amuck to that of homosexuality.

There is a second element of male sexuality apropos to sources cited by Furnish for elaborating the sexual perspectives of Paul.[18] That is the pattern of portraying the one penetrated (in male homosexual acts) as serving the female role. Obviously, there is a biological dimension to this portrayal, and one could insist that this is all that lies underneath the ascription of femininity to the role of the penetrated. But in the passages adduced by Furnish to illustrate Greco-Roman sexual attitudes contemporaneous with Paul, it can be reasonably argued that the moral disapproval expressed toward the homosexual act arises specifically from male perception of the female role on the part of what is so frequently designated the "passive" partner. That is to say, the succumbent party threatens manhood by abandoning the position of masculine dominance. Furnish cites Plutarch's *Dialogue on Love* (751D, E) wherein Daphnaeus attacks involuntary homosexual intercourse on grounds of its violence and then proceeds to denounce such intercourse even when voluntary, because "there is still weakness and effeminacy on the part of those who, contrary to nature, allow themselves in Plato's

[17]Mary Daly, *Beyond God the Father* (Boston: Beacon Press, 1973), pp. 114–22. Also, in *The Casualties of War* (New York: McGraw-Hill, 1969), Daniel Lang recounts the kidnapping, rape, and murder of a young Viet girl by an American patrol in Vietnam in 1966. In the taxonomy of sexual mayhem the episode naturally falls in the same class with Gibeah or Sodom.

[18]For what follows, see also Beverly W. Harrison, "Misogyny and Homophobia: The Unexplored Connections," *Church and Society* 72 (November/December 1982):20–33.

words 'to be mounted like cattle.' "[19] This statement expresses misogyny with the words weakness and effeminacy and in the use of the cattle analogy.[20] The same demeaning of the female role is in a Philo passage on Sodom cited by Furnish:

> Not only in their mad lust for women did they violate the marriages of their neighbors, but also men mounted males without respect for the sex nature which the active partner shares with the passive; and so when they tried to beget children they were discovered to be incapable of any but a sterile seed. Yet the discovery availed them not, so much stronger was the force of the lust which mastered them. Then, as little by little they accustomed those who were by nature men to submit to play the part of women, they saddled them with the formidable curse of a female disease.[21]

Philo goes on to say in this same context that if Greek and barbarian homosexuality had continued, "city after city would have become a desert, as though depopulated by a pestilential sickness," but God blessed heterosexual marriage with fertility and "extinguished this unnatural and forbidden intercourse." The assigned female part in intercourse, procreation, and divine blessing is fixed. Although Philo's biology is somewhat opaque in the whole passage, sterility seems to result directly from homosexual acts. Venereal disease (not connected by Philo with sterility) is misogynously designated a "female disease" communicated (as divine judgment?) to those who "play the part of women" by those who play the part of men.[22]

[19] Plutarch *Dialogue on Love*, 751 D, E, in vol. 9 of Plutarch's *Moralia*, trans. W.C. Helmbold, Loeb Classical Library (Cambridge, MA: Harvard University Press, 1961), p. 323.

[20] This misogyny is not confined to male heterosexuals. Lesbian ministers of the Metropolitan Community Church speak of problems of male dominance in their congregation. See also Jeffrey Weeks, *Coming Out* (New York: Quartet, 1977), pp. 196–203, 213, on the struggle by women against masculine rule in the gay/lesbian liberation movement.

[21] Philo, *On Abraham*, 135–36, in vol. 6 of Philo, trans. F.H. Colson, Loeb Classical Library (Cambridge, MA: Harvard University Press, 1935), p. 71.

[22] Morton S. Enslin, *The Ethics of Paul* (New York: Harper & Bros. (1930), p. 147, n. 45, perceived in "due penalty for their error" at Romans 1:27 a reference to venereal disease. This naturalistic interpretation of Paul would seem to be more at home in Philo's philosophy than in Paul, even if Philo's biology is fantastic from the modern standpoint. Once medicine is able, through prophylaxis, to break the cause-effect relationship between wrongdoing and the divine retribution it provokes, the end of that theology is at hand and the end of a religion that makes that view of God integral to its belief. Note, however, that the lethal acquired immunity deficiency syndrome (AIDS) that was first reported in *The New York Times*, July 3, 1981, had claimed about 1,850 gay deaths (out of 3,700 cases) by spring 1984. Despite encouraging progress in diagnosis, no effective medical preventive had been developed. Further comment is found on pp. 117–19.

Although Philo does not use the term *malakos* ("weak," "effeminate") in this passage to refer to the "passive" partner, Furnish finds this distinction (passive/active) in 1 Corinthians 6:9, and Philo uses his own vocabulary *(paschein/dran)* for the same idea. Masculine power is expressed in this formulation, and Dover[23] has given considerable attention to the parallel in Greek sexuality between the derogation of females and the derogation of the passive homosexual role in language obviously expressive of a common androcentric denominator. Furnish is not unaware that in contemporary moral language description of the passive role may often be a device for conveying homophobic attitudes; but I am suggesting that this awareness belongs etiologically with the power of patriarchy not only in Greco-Roman philosophy but also in the thought of Paul.

Herant Katchadourian and Donald Lunde have commented on the frequently encountered preoccupation with the assignment of active and passive roles to persons engaged in homosexual acts. They report on a clinical study of such roles that showed that only 20 percent of the total sample "could be said to show distinct preferences for given activities, as well as particular roles." Homosexuals, they observe, may "switch roles during a sex act," and they conclude:

> Despite these findings, important conclusions continue to be drawn from such spurious distinctions. Some psychiatrists, for instance, attempt to link such distinctions to character traits and histories of psycho-sexual development. Judges tend to be harsher with "active" partners. Homosexuals themselves are no exception: Some men, in fact, claim that they are not homosexual at all because they exercise exclusively "masculine roles" in their encounters with other men.[24]

The meaning of the adjective *malakoi* translated in conjunction with the noun *arsenokoitai* as "homosexuals" in the first edition of the RSV at 1 Corinthians 6:9 is of much interest to Furnish and Boswell in understanding Paul's attitude toward homosexuality as well as the impact of this vocabulary on the attitudes of the churches. By interfacing the expositions of these two writers one is led into additional dimensions of the liberationist perspective.

[23] Kenneth J. Dover, *Greek Homosexuality* (Cambridge, MA: Harvard University Press, 1978), pp. 52, 67–68.
[24] Herant A. Katchadourian and Donald T. Lunde, *Fundamentals of Human Sexuality*, 2d ed. (New York: Holt, Rinehart & Winston, 1975), p. 327. These writers provide the appropriate response to Dover's emphasis on roles.

FURNISH AND BOSWELL ON THE LEXICOGRAPHY OF
1 CORINTHIANS 6:9

Furnish renders 1 Corinthians 6:9 containing the two words *malakoi* and *arsenokoitai:* "nor men who assume the female role in sex, nor men who have sex with them."[25] Except for Furnish's commendable avoidance of "sodomites," this translation is similar to that of the *Jerusalem Bible,* "catamites" and "sodomites" (presumed to signify "penetrated" and "penetrators").

Boswell suggests "unrestrained" or "wanton" for the first of these words but insists that it does not refer to gay men or to same-sex acts.[26] For *arsenokoitai,* Boswell prefers "male prostitutes," not to be construed as "male *cult* prostitutes" or male prostitutes who served other males.[27] As a summary, Boswell states: "There is no reason to believe that either *arsenokoitai* or *malakoi* connoted homosexuality in the time of Paul or for centuries thereafter, and every reason to suppose that, whatever they came to mean, they were not determinative of Christian opinion or the morality of homosexual acts."[28]

The two translators obviously diverge in their sense of what Paul is saying, even though Furnish admits that "one cannot be absolutely certain that the two key words in 1 Corinthians 6:9 are meant as references to male homosexual behavior."[29] The intent of the following discussion is not to vindicate Boswell's position without qualification but to refine it from a theological and methodological standpoint in order to secure more adequately its liberationist moorings.

Boswell addresses himself to the first edition of the RSV which uses "homosexuals" for the two words in question.[30] In the second edition of 1971, however, the RSV reverted to "sexual perverts," and that should have been the point of discussion in his 1980 book. The revised reading is probably as unacceptable to Boswell as the earlier one, but the revisers may have provided opportunity for interpreters to point out that "perverse" applied to both heterosexuals and homosexuals who violated their natural orientation or preference, without condemning homosexuals as such.

[25] *Moral Teaching of Paul,* p. 70.
[26] John Boswell, *Christianity, Social Tolerance, and Homosexuality* (Chicago: University of Chicago Press, 1980), p. 107.
[27] Ibid., pp. 107; 345, n. 25.
[28] Ibid., p. 353.
[29] Furnish, *Moral Teaching of Paul,* p. 73.
[30] *Christianity, Social Tolerance, and Homosexuality,* p. 338.

Boswell cites Matthew 11:8 as an example of *malakos* meaning "sick."[31] In this text *malakos* refers twice to "clothing" (implied but not expressed in the Greek) and means "soft" in the literal sense or, contextually, something like "luxurious." In the same note, Boswell cites 4:23; 9:35; and 10:1 for comparison; but these texts use *malakia* ("sickness"), not *malakos*, and are not relevant to 1 Corinthians 6:9. In fact, nowhere in the New Testament does *malakos* mean "sick," as Boswell's note would imply.

Boswell claims that *arsenokoitēs* at 1 Corinthians 6:9 and 1 Timothy 1:10 (the only occurrences of this word in the New Testament) means "male fucker"—the Greek word has a vulgar connotation—rather than "fucker of males" and applies not to same-sex intercourse between males but to intercourse between males and females.[32] This is premised on the assertion that copulation with other males would have been expressed with "arreno-" rather than "arsenokoitēs." This argument runs aground on the fact that the spellings *arr-* and *ars-* occur without differentiation in the Oxyrhynchus Papyri, in the Zenon Papyri, and in manuscripts of biblical Greek. Dover is confident that -rr- is Attic spelling and -rs- is normal for other dialects, including Hellenistic Greek.[33] It must be added too that Boswell's discussion of the letters of Paul assumes Pauline authorship of the Pastoral Epistles (1 and 2 Timothy; Titus) and even of Hebrews[34]—an assumption negated by Furnish, presumably because of his recognition that the vocabulary, theology, and morality of the Deutero-Pauline literature moves away from the distinctiveness of Paul. Careful study of the Pastorals reveals that words or phrases in them, which also appear in the undisputed letters, may be used in a recognizably different way.

Boswell's willingness to question translators and lexicographers, however, must not be dismissed as futile. For reasons already observed in Gunkel's view of Genesis 19, Boswell correctly repudiates Luther's rendering of *arsenokoitai* as *Knabenschänder* ("child molesters").[35] It is also true in broad terms that the association of *malakos* (meaning "soft," "effeminate") with homosexuality is frequently erroneous and may well be homophobic.[36] The standard

---

[31] Ibid., p. 106, n. 49.
[32] Ibid., pp. 342–44.
[33] By letter to author, dated October 26, 1982.
[34] *Christianity, Social Tolerance, and Homosexuality,* pp. 101, n. 36; 104; 106.
[35] Ibid., p. 338, n. 7.
[36] Ibid., pp. 107, 339.

current lexicon for New Testament Greek is the work of Walter Bauer, F.W. Gingrich, and F.W. Danker.[37] Under evidence that *malakos* means "catamite" at 1 Corinthians 6:9 are cited Papyrus Hibeh 54,11 and a passage from Adolf Deissmann's *Licht vom Osten* (4th ed., p. 130). These references deserve closer scrutiny.

Hibeh letter 54 from the well-off householder Demophon to the police official Ptolemaios contains instructions about the provision of musicians for a pending celebration at the house of Demophon. Bernard Grenfell and Arthur Hunt date the letter about 245 B.C. The line in question asks for the dispatch of Zenobius the *malakos*, presumably a musician, to perform in the appointed fest. Grenfell and Hunt render the sentence as follows: "Send me also Zenobius the effeminate with a drum and cymbals and castanets, for he is wanted by the women for the sacrifice, and let him wear as fine clothes as possible."[38] The word effeminate, translating *malakos*, has the following footnote: "*Malakos* may be merely a nickname, but probably refers to the style of Zenobius' dancing. Smyly well compares Plautus, Mil 668 *Tum ad saltandum non cinaedus malacus aequest atque ego.*"

It is clear in the first place that nothing in line 11 or the whole of the Hibeh letter 54 demonstrates that Zenobius was a catamite, either professionally or occasionally. Nor can it be shown from Plautus, Mil. 668 that this is so. The Plautus passage does bring together *cinaedus* (Latin for Greek *kinaidos*, "catamite") and *malacus* (Greek, *malakos*). Paul Nixon, with Victorian euphemisms, translates thus: "And from the self-same source (tapping his chest) I'll produce for you the gayest of dinner guests, or a peerless parasite, yes, and an incomparable caterer. And as for the dancing, there's no professional (pirouetting) can step it so seductively as I."[39] The last sentence translates line 668, *Tum ad saltandum non cinaedus malacus aequest atque ego.* More literally, this can be read: "Then at dancing, there is no catamite so nimble as I am." This rendering correctly shows that *malacus* is not a synonym of *cinaedus*

[37] Walter Bauer, F.W. Gingrich, and F.W. Danker, *A Greek-English Lexicon of the New Testament*, 2d ed. (Chicago: University of Chicago Press, 1979), p. 488.

[38] Bernard P. Grenfell and Arthur S. Hunt, eds., *The Hibeh Papyrus*, pt. 1 (London: Kegan Paul, French, Trübner, 1906), p. 201. Robin Scroggs, in *The New Testament and Homosexuality* (Philadelphia: Fortress Press, 1983), p. 64, correctly comments: "Nothing in the brief letter makes any suggestion of pederasty."

[39] Plautus, *The Braggart Warrior*, in vol. 3 of Plautus, trans. Paul Nixon, Loeb Classical Library (New York: G.P. Putnam's Sons, 1924), p. 193.

but a predicate modifier of it. Karl Georges cites this text from Plautus and gives its contextual meaning as *gelenkig,* "nimble."[40] So the Plautus passage is useless for showing that *malakos* at 1 Corinthians 6:9 means "catamite."

Grenfell and Hunt do not discuss 1 Corinthians 6:9 in connection with the Hibeh letter of Demophon to Ptolemaios, but Deissmann does. Concerning the adjective *malakos* attached to Zenobius the musician, he says: "The word is no doubt used in its secondary (obscene) sense, as by St. Paul in 1 Cor vi.9. It is an allusion to the foul practises by which the musician eked out his earnings."[41] We learn from this declaration that we are led into a circular argument. Bauer appeals to Papyrus Hibeh and its treatment in Deissmann to show that *malakos* means "catamite" in 1 Corinthians 6:9, but since Deissmann appeals to 1 Corinthians 6:9 to show that the word has this meaning in Papyrus Hibeh, the conclusion already reached is adduced as proof of it! The linkup with Plautus, Mil. 668, attributed to Smyly by Grenfell and Hunt, is also supported by Bauer and enters the circle of confusion between presumption and proof.

Bauer also cites Dio Chrysostom 66.25 to confirm the use of "catamites" at 1 Corinthians 6:9. In this passage the philosopher is warning against paying attention to the foolish talk of the crowd, expanding on a line from Homer, "blunt the missile of a feeble good-for-naught." In a series of examples that show what groundless taunts are apt to be hurled, Dio writes: "If you are always rushing into the marketplace, you will hear yourself called a market idler and a shyster, whereas, if, on the contrary, you are wary of that sort of thing and keep more at home and attend to your own affairs, you will be called simple-minded and effeminate."[42] Again the final word translates *malakos.* Although the context shows that nothing complimentary is meant by "effeminate," it is equally certain that the notion of catamite does not arise from the passage itself but must be read into it by the presupposition of the reader.

These examples from Papyrus Hibeh, Deissmann, Grenfell and Hunt, Plautus, and Dio Chrysostom show that Bauer's treatment of *malakos* is not beyond reproach. The case for reading "catamite" at

[40] Karl E. Georges und Heinrich Georges, Hrsg., *Lateinisch-Deutsches Handwörterbuch,* 11. Aufl., 2. Bd. (Basel: Benno Schwabe, 1962), col. 775.

[41] Adolf Deissman, *Light from the Ancient East,* trans. L.R.M. Strachan, rev. ed. (London: Hodder and Stoughton, 1927), p. 164, n. 4.

[42] Dio Chrysostom, *Discourses,* vol. 5, trans. H. Lamar Crosby, Loeb Classical Library (Cambridge, MA: Harvard University Press, 1951), pp. 110–13.

1 Corinthians 6:9 is far less secure than a glance at Bauer would indicate. Boswell further senses the essential conflict between Paul's understanding of liberty in Galatians and attitudes of legal rectitude arising from ethnic or hieratic propriety,[43] and his citing of Titus 1:14–15 in this regard could be easily improved by appeal to Romans 14:14, an unmistakably Pauline text that expresses the same idea.

One thing is morally certain and must be underlined. The stereotyping of homosexuals as effeminate is prejudicial. Heterosexuals may be effeminate (whatever the standard for such a designation) and homosexual males may be very masculine (muscular, athletic, etc.) by popular measurements.[44]

Moltmann-Wendel appropriately emphasizes that in washing the disciples' feet (narrated only in John 13) Jesus assumed an intimate function usually performed by a woman for her husband.[45] The masculine prescription is again broken by Jesus in John 4:27. Because contemporary stereotypes of what is effeminate are often prejudicial and in general serve purposes of social hierarchy, it is reasonable to expect that ancient perceptions were not free of these same tendencies, and Boswell's protestations are, in general, salutary and edifying.

ROMANS 1:26–27 IN LIBERATIONIST PERSPECTIVE

The importance of Romans in New Testament theology is axiomatic, particularly in Protestantism. Because it extends and reiterates many of the earlier emphases of Paul's thought, its elegant formulations of Christian belief exercise a somewhat controlling and normative role over the interpretation of the entire Pauline corpus. The importance of Romans is heightened in respect to the theology of gay/lesbian liberation by the fact that the Gospels do not explicitly refer to homosexual conduct. Romans 1:26 is initially distinguished by containing the only reference in all of scripture to lesbian behavior. Until a more persuasive explanation is brought forth, I conclude that this omission should be attributed to biblical androcentricity both in the sense that female conduct usually falls outside the pur-

---

[43]*Christianity, Social Tolerance, and Homosexuality*, p. 104.

[44]Katchadourian and Lunde, *Fundamentals of Human Sexuality*, p. 325.

[45]Moltmann-Wendel, *Liberty, Equality, Sisterhood*, p. 33. Cf. C.K. Barrett, *The Gospel According to St. John*, 2d ed. (Philadelphia: Westminster Press, 1978), p. 440.

view of moral legislation (cf. the tenth commandment) and in the sense that female homosexuality does not directly imply the abandonment of male power.

In my commentary on Romans 1:26f. I will proceed along three lines of investigation: the theological world view it reflects; the traditional linkage, idolatry-adultery-homosexuality; and the contextual significance of the verses in the whole of Romans.

1. *The theological world view of Romans 1:26–27.* A thematic statement about the revelation of the wrath of God against all ungodliness introduces the section, Romans 1:18–32. It is difficult to avoid the impression that verse 18 places us once again in the presence of the fire-and-brimstone God of the Jahwist, with corresponding assumptions regarding the relation of this God to the cosmic order. Romans 1:26f. stands in the middle of a threefold repetition of the expression "God gave them up" (in vss. 24, 26, and 28), and the use of connective conjunctions at verses 24 and 26 makes one feel that the wrath of God is being manifested throughout this section. The theological world view underlying the passage is, therefore, ridden with problems for contemporary theological reflection, so that with much reason Paul Tillich was led to comment on the concept of the wrath of God:

> Christian theologians have both used and criticized the term. Criticism has usually recalled that in paganism the concept of the "anger of the gods" presupposes the idea of a finite God whose emotions can be aroused by other finite beings. Such a concept obviously contradicts the divinity of the divine and its unconditional character. Therefore, the concept has to be reinterpreted or completely abandoned in Christian thought.[46]

It will be subsequently argued that Paul presents in this section not thoughts that proceed from his own understanding of divine justice but those of Jewish tradition looking out in a customary way on gentile depravity. Before that, however, it must be said that Tillich's statement of the problem and the solution proposed to it are profoundly instructive for biblical theology, if Tillich's sugges-

[46]Paul Tillich, *Systematic Theology*, vol. 2 (Chicago: University of Chicago Press, 1962), pp. 76–77. In accord with his subjectivism and categories of psychology, Tillich further holds that the symbol of "the wrath of God" reflects the experience of despair. This is meaningful but needs to be extended to social and political categories.

tion is allowed to direct us in the repressive use that religious establishments have historically made of the wrath of God.

Sensitive to the profound moral problems inherent in the angry deity concept, C.H. Dodd commented in the days of liberalism that Paul frequently writes "*the* wrath" but only once or twice uses the expression "the wrath of God."[47] Dodd was followed in this suggestion by A.T. Hanson[48] and G.H.C. Macgregor,[49] among others. *The New English Bible,* tending toward an impersonalization of the symbol, uses "divine retribution" at Romans 1:18 and 12:19 but usually "retribution" at the much more frequent occurrences (e.g., Romans 2:5, 8; 3:5; 4:15; 5:9; 9:22a (his retribution); 9:22b; 13:4, 5, etc.). In more recent, antiliberal times, however, there has been a disposition to restore the directness of God's agency in the apocalyptic mode of thought in which Paul here expresses himself, and repudiations of Dodd's desire to impersonalize the wrath have come into vogue. As representatives of this more current trend, we could name Ernst Käsemann,[50] Ulrich Mauser,[51] and John Murray.[52] If one insists, however, that Paul's very own understanding is at work in phrases that speak of "the wrath of God" and how "God gave them up," one is thrust back into the embarrassing process of explaining God's agency in the mayhem and misery that characterize human existence and fall without distinction on the lives of the saints. Not least among the difficulties arising from the notion of God's wrath is the comprehension of the death of Christ on behalf of sinners, the *iustificatio impii,* which is expressed in Romans 5:8–9 and is the soul of Paul's gospel. In those verses the love of God comes to expression in the death of Christ that saves us from "the wrath." Even here many of the older translations insisted on saying "the wrath of God," giving rise to a grotesque notion of God's love acting in and on Christ's death to deliver us (by appeasement?) from God's wrath. In

[47] C.H. Dodd, *The Epistle of Paul to the Romans,* Moffatt New Testament Commentary (1932; London: Hodder and Stoughton, 1947), pp. 20–24.

[48] A.T. Hanson, *The Wrath of the Lamb* (London: SPCK, 1957).

[49] G.H.C. Macgregor, "The Concept of the Wrath of God in the New Testament," *New Testament Studies* 7 (1960/61):101–9.

[50] Käsemann, *Commentary on Romans,* p. 37.

[51] Ulrich Mauser, *Gottesbild und Menschwerdung,* Beiträge zur historischen Theologie 43 (Tübingen: J.C.B. Mohr, 1971), pp. 148–51.

[52] John Murray, *The Epistle to the Romans,* New International Commentary on the New Testament (Grand Rapids, MI: Wm. B. Eerdmans, 1959), pp. 44–45.

some incomprehensible way this was supposed to represent the hidden mystery of God's dealing with human waywardness. One need only remember the wreckage wrought by torture, by penal systems, and by warfare, carried out by human beings considering themselves agents of divine wrath, in order to test the social consequences of this theologoumenon. So Käsemann must himself resort to an impersonalization of the wrath in commenting on Romans 5:9 that God's love is "the almighty power which effects salvation, brings forth the creation out of nothing *(creatio ex nihilo)*, and puts an end to wrath."[53]

The theology of gay/lesbian liberation calls for an end to a fire-and-brimstone God who designates homosexuals as objects of divine anger. The search for Sodom and Gomorrah belongs on a par with the search for remains of Noah's ark, with equally negligible results. Thomas Thompson has found unconvincing the thesis of W.F. Albright that the Cities of the Plain (Genesis 14:3) were Middle Bronze I settlements (2100–1900 B.C.) now submerged at the southern end of the Dead Sea.[54] Despite J.P. Harlan's admission that no archeological traces of Sodom and Gomorrah have been found, the desire to historicize the saga persists in Harlan's belief that "the sites may with great probability be located in the area now submerged under the waters of the southern part of the Dead Sea."[55] Theology must, however, recognize that even if the Dead Sea silt should eventually yield some tangible sign of natural calamity that incinerated ancient cities of the area, the discussion of such a calamity must be carried out in a time when mythological pronouncements concerning divine beings are subjected to sociological analysis and the transmutations that social forces impose on religious ideas.

Healthy, morally discreet homosexuals recognize instinctively the oppression that lurks behind the symbol of the wrath of God and, like Job, reject the condemnation that pious counselors seek to impart on the basis of it. They recognize already, as Boswell emphasizes,[56] that Romans 1:26f. could not apply to those naturally disposed to homosexuality but to those naturally heterosexual who

[53] Käsemann, *Commentary on Romans*, p. 138.
[54] Thomas L. Thompson, *The Historicity of the Patriarchal Narratives*, Beiheft zu Zeitschrift für die alttestamentliche Wissenschaft 133 (New York: Walter de Gruyter, 1974), p. 174.
[55] J.P. Harlan, "Sodom," *Interpreter's Dictionary of the Bible*, R–Z:396.
[56] Boswell, *Christianity, Social Tolerance, and Homosexuality*, p. 109. Furnish, *Moral Teaching of Paul*, p. 81, agrees obliquely.

engage in homosexual practices. Job, as Ernst Bloch emphasizes,[57] was a type of biblical Prometheus, a gigantic resister of religious conventionalisms, pointing forward to the deliverer. The irreligion or atheism of many homosexuals roots in their refusal to accept the misdirected moral condemnation by which biblical pietists, instructed by what they perceive to be the wrath of God, seek the psychological, legal, and social incineration of lesbians and gays. Like Job, the prophets, or Jesus himself, who learned by bitter experience to distinguish God from sanctimonious misrepresentations, the liberated homosexual may well renew for us once again the power of prayer and the significance of believing.

2. *Paul's use of the idolatry-adultery-homosexuality tradition.* In the foregoing discussion of the theological world view of Romans 1:26f., it can reasonably be questioned from the standpoint of historical exegesis whether the fire-and-brimstone Jahweh of Genesis 19 is consciously present in Paul's portrayal of the God of wrath in Romans 1. The response to this is that once historical exegesis assumes moral and social responsibility for what the text means now as well as what it meant in a specific religious situation of the first century,[58] the question that arises from the experience of the modern interrogator of the text is not only permissible but necessary for our religious sanity. This is further confirmed by an examination of the traditional threefold depiction (idolatry-adultery-homosexuality) of gentile depravity common to 1 Corinthians 6:9–10 and Romans 1:18–32.

The first of these can be briefly and simply put. Paul writes: "Do not be deceived; neither the immoral, nor idolaters, nor adulterers,

---

[57] Ernst Bloch, *Das Prinzip Hoffnung*, Kapitel 38–55, Gesamtausgabe Bd. 5 (Frankfurt am Main: Suhrkamp, 1959), p. 1456, describes Job's faith in this manner: "The Exodus is in Job radicalized: not merely as a measurement of God by the ideal of his righteousness and of his righteous kingdom, but as *Exodus out of Jahwe himself* into the unknown Canaan, the promise of which he had not fulfilled. 'I know my avenger lives and will at last arise over my dust. The witness of my innocence will be with me, and I will see my redeemer for myself, I, with my own eyes, and no other' (Job 19:25–27 according to the translation of Bertholet, with the use of conjectural readings). The messianic belief of this text, handed down not without reason in a corrupted form, even leaves Jahwe behind—for the sake of his utopia. But if Moses had not preached God in Canaan, Canaan in God, Job had possessed neither language for his complaint nor light for his rebellious hope."

[58] In biblical theology the text should not be deprived of its future. Cf. Krister Stendahl, "Biblical Theology, Contemporary," *Interpreter's Dictionary of the Bible*, A–D:419.

nor sexual perverts, nor thieves, nor the greedy, nor drunkards, nor revilers, nor robbers will inherit the kingdom of God [1 Cor 6:9b–10]." I will not repeat here questions associated with the *Revised Standard Version* rendering of two Greek words by the one expression, "sexual perverts." What is to be noted in this context is that the first four entities of the list connect idolatry, adultery (or sexual immorality), and sexual perversion. Furnish correctly clarifies the RSV "immoral" by translating "sexually immoral."[59] It is, further, a standard observation that vice lists of this type are standard in Greco-Roman moral philosophy of a popular sort,[60] with the exception of the attack on idolatry. When these lists were taken up in Jewish and then in Christian moral exhortation, idolatry was given a prominent place, baptizing the material, so to speak, for use in the monotheistic culture.[61]

As to Romans 1:26f., it is Gunkel himself who describes its pertinence to the exegesis of Genesis 19 and the fate of Sodom:

> Even the sin of this ancient city the saga knows precisely; it was unnatural lust, the sin of Canaan. On account of this sin, which they were even willing to practise on the Deity, this city was destroyed. It is characteristic for Israel's experience that this lust is spoken of with such gravity. In testimony of it there is an uninterrupted series of documents from the earliest time down to Rom 1:26f.[62]

When Gunkel speaks of an "uninterrupted series of documents from the earliest time down to Rom 1:26f." he not only includes Leviticus 18:22 and 20:13 but also presumably intends references to Sodom and abominations in the prophets, as well as in the intertestamental literature.[63]

My inquiry into Sodom among the prophets did not concur in all aspects of Gunkel's generalization, and his introduction of child molestation into the Genesis account was found to be fantastic. I argued that in Ezekiel and Hosea particularly the interweaving of

---

[59] Furnish, *Moral Teaching of Paul*, p. 70.

[60] Furnish, *Theology and Ethics in Paul* (Nashville: Abingdon Press, 1968), pp. 71–92. Furnish emphasizes that Paul took up secular moral instruction including the lists, along with Judaistic and earlier Christian parenesis but adapted these to his particular ecclesiastical tasks.

[61] Ehrhard Kamlah, *Die Form der katalogischen Paränese im Neuen Testament*, Wissenschaftliche Untersuchungen zum Neuen Testament 7 (Tübingen: J.C.B. Mohr, 1964), pp. 177–78. B.S. Easton, "New Testament Ethical Lists," *Journal of Biblical Literature* 51 (1932):4.

[62] Gunkel, *Genesis*, p. 215.

[63] Ibid., p. 108.

idolatry and sexual immorality was evident, whereas sexual perversion, the third member of the triadic tradition, was lacking. I also hold that phallic aggression is a more significant characterization of Sodom's fault than presuppositions about the cult of Canaan nowhere explicit in the text of Genesis 19. In the Deuteronomic history, however, there is evidence of the threefold constellation portending national disaster. That the inclusion of homosexual acts in addition to the first two attested in the prophets (idolatry and adultery) persisted in intertestamental literature is shown in the Book of Wisdom.

Like all learned commentators on Romans 1:18–32, Furnish adduces the Wisdom of Solomon as the primary background of Paul's thought in this section.[64] Furnish begins his remarks by saying: "In 1:18–32 the Apostle is denouncing the wickedness of the Gentiles in terms and with arguments that were the stock-in-trade of much Hellenistic Jewish teaching." From Wisdom 13:1–19, Furnish proceeds to show that these verses parallel Romans 1:18ff. in ways that are too decisive to be treated as accidental. For example, the knowledge of God is readily accessible from the greatness and beauty of created things (Wisdom 13:1,5; Romans 1:20); gentiles do search for and obtain a certain knowledge of God (Wisdom 13:6–7; Romans 1:21); but they still fall short of genuine knowledge of God and are without excuse (Wisdom 13:8–9; Romans 1:21); they worship stars as well as idols they themselves have carved and painted, and this is ultimate folly (Wisdom 13:2, 13–19; Romans 1:21–23, 25). From Wisdom 11:15–20 and 12:17 we learn that as a result of worshiping "irrational serpents and worthless animals" (cf. Romans 1:23) punishment ensues, not in an impersonal or automatic way, but is sent by God just as Paul speaks of God's wrath (Romans 1:18) and God "giving them up" (Romans 1:24, 26, 28). The most important parallel for our present discussion emerges from Wisdom 14:12–27. Verse 12 reads:

> For the idea of making idols was
> the beginning of fornication
> and the invention of them was the
> corruption of life.

Here we meet the inclusive assertion (reiterated in Wisdom 14:27) that idolatry is the root evil, immediately linked to fornication. We

---

[64] Furnish, *Moral Teaching of Paul*, pp. 74–78.

must wait until Wisdom 14:26 before the appearance of the third element of the triad, sex perversion, appears in a list of vices reminiscent in literary form at least of Romans 1:29–31.[65] The RSV translates Wisdom 14:24–26 as follows:

> [24]they no longer keep either their
> lives or their marriages pure,
> but they either treacherously kill
> one another, or grieve one
> another by adultery.
> [25]and all is a raging riot of blood and
> murder, theft and deceit,
> corruption, faithlessness, tumult,
> perjury
> [26]confusion over what is good,
> forgetfulness of favors,
> pollution of idols, sex perversion,
> disorder in marriage, adultery,
> and debauchery.

Turning once again to Romans 1:18–32, the threefold mark of gentile depravity comes forth in verses 22–27: Verse 23 describes their idolatry; verse 24 tells of God giving them up to sexual sins[66]; verses 26f. speak of God giving them up to sexual perversion.

To summarize, in the two specific references to same-sex acts in the letters of Paul, they are united with a root cause, idolatry and fornication or adultery. These three components are found in Hellenistic Judaism, especially the Wisdom of Solomon, which is a storehouse of ideas that crop up in Romans 1:18–32 and elsewhere in Romans. The same three ingredients are also attested in the Deuteronomic history. Paul, therefore, is utilizing a tradition, a tradition especially characterized by Judaism's perspective on gentile depravity. The critical question is, How does Paul regard this threefold tradition? Is it taken up at face value, uncritically, or does Paul use it rhetorically in order to gain the assent of the Jewish

[65]Only two words, murder (phonos) and deceit (dolos), are common to the fifteen-term list in Wisdom and the twenty-one term list in Romans.

[66]Moffatt rendered verse 24: "So God has given them up, in their heart's lust to sexual vice, to the dishonoring of their bodies." C.K. Barrett, A Commentary on the Epistle to the Romans, Harper's New Testament Commentaries (New York: Harper & Bros., 1957), p. 38, finds "sexual" (or homosexual) passions in verse 24. Heinrich Schlier, Der Römerbrief, Herders theologischer Kommentar zum Neuen Testament (Freiburg: Herder, 1977), p. 59, finds in the noun akatharsia (vs. 24) sexual licentiousness in attitude and deed.

boaster whose judgment against the gentiles becomes his own condemnation in Romans 2? In this final section the view is maintained that Romans 1:26–27 stands in a rhetorical context wherein Paul uses a traditional Jewish pattern of ideas directed against gentile depravity in order to turn the accusation against the accuser, just as the prophets turned the ethnocentric accusations against the Canaanites in on Israel itself and gave rise thereby to the moral depth of prophetic religion. In this manner heterosexuality, particularly male heterosexuality, is called into judgment against itself on the basis of homosexual inclusion that faith justification implies. Insofar as Paul's sexuality does not carry out this freedom-based-on-faith, the theology of gay/lesbian liberation requires its correction, just as Galatians 3:28 must be used as the norm and corrective of elements of patriarchy in Paul not consonant with it.

3. *Contextual significance of Romans 1:26–27 in the whole of Romans.* Furnish concludes his correlation of Romans 1:18–32 with Wisdom 11—14 with the following statement: "The pattern of thought in Romans 1:18–32 should now be clear. It is a denunciation of the Gentiles formulated in accord with traditional Jewish reasoning."[67] One must now ask: Does Paul join in this denunciation? Is he at one with the mood of the Book of Wisdom? To stand in the shoes of Wisdom would be most unlike Paul, I hold, and essentially at odds with Paul's own fierce sense of gentile inclusion on the basis of faith alone.

Hans Lietzmann correctly adduces Wisdom 15:1ff. to explain the logic of Romans 2:1ff.[68] In the former passage the Jewish author of Wisdom voices the confidence that although the circumcised may sin (an unlikely eventuality), their sin is something different from gentile sin because they are not idolators and, despite such sin, stand in special relation to God. The pertinent verses run thus: "But thou, our God, art kind and true, patient, and ruling all things in mercy. For even if we sin we are thine, knowing thy power; but we

[67] Furnish, *Moral Teaching of Paul*, p. 77.

[68] Hans Lietzmann, *An die Römer*, 5. Aufl., Handbuch zum Neuen Testament, hrsg. v. G. Bornkamm (Tübingen: J.C.B. Mohr, 1971), pp. 38–39. Anders Nygren, *Commentary on Romans*, trans. Carl C. Rasmussen (Philadelphia: Muhlenberg Press, 1949), pp. 114–15, has essentially the same view. Käsemann, *Commentary on Romans*, pp. 53–54, begins his exposition of Romans 2:1–11 by saying it "can be understood only as a polemic against the Jewish tradition which comes out most clearly and with much the same vocabulary in Wis 15:1ff."

will not sin, because we know that we are accounted thine. . . . **For**
neither has the evil intent of human art misled us, nor the fruitless
toil of painters, a figure stained with various colors [Wis. 15:1–2,
4]."

It is clear, of course, that the Jewish boaster is expressly mentioned at Romans 2:17ff., but major commentators now recognize
that also at 2:1ff. the attitude comparable to that in Wisdom 15:1ff. is
brought under attack. So Heinrich Schlier says in reference to Romans 2:1: "Exegesis is today rather unanimously clear that Paul
already has the Jew in view here."[69] William Manson has emphasized that the latter part of Romans 1 is dominated by the pronoun
they or them.[70] "What can be known about God is plain to *them* [vs.
19]"; *"they* are without excuse [vs. 20]"; "although *they* knew God
they did not honor [God] as God [vs. 21]"; *"they* became futile in
their thinking and *their* senseless minds were darkened [vs. 21]";
"they became fools [vs. 22]"; and so on. Romans 2 suddenly shifts,
however, to the second person: "*You* have no excuse . . . whoever
you are, when *you* judge another; for in passing judgment upon him
you condemn *yourself,* because *you,* the judge, are doing the very
same things." Is not the purpose of this sudden change of pronouns
at Romans 2:1 part of the rhetorical function that is served by all of
Romans 1:18–32, namely, to set up (for indictment) the chauvinistic
reader who is already under address in chapter 1? William Sanday
and H.C. Headlam comment on the shift at Romans 2:1:

> The transition from Gentile to Jew is conducted with much rhetorical
> skill, somewhat after the manner of Nathan's parable to David. Under
> cover of a general statement St. Paul sets before himself a typical Jew.
> Such an one would assent cordially to all that had been said
> hitherto. . . . It is now turned against himself, though for the moment
> the Apostle holds in suspense the direct affirmation, "Thou art the
> man!"[71]

Other examples of this rhetorical maneuver exist in biblical literature besides the Nathan parable in 2 Samuel 12:1–7. Amos 1 and 2
may be cited. There the prophet elicits the Hebrew reader's ap-

[69] Schlier, *Der Römerbrief,* p. 68. Likewise, Günther Bornkamm, *Early Christian
Experience,* trans. Paul L. Hammer (New York: Harper & Row, 1969), p. 69, n. 54.

[70] William Manson, *The Epistle to the Hebrews* (London: Hodder and Stoughton,
1951), p. 174.

[71] William Sanday and H.C. Headlam, *A Critical and Exegetical Commentary on
the Epistle to the Romans,* 5th ed., International Critical Commentary (Edinburgh:
T & T Clark, 1902), p. 54.

proval of his condemnation of Damascus (1:3), Gaza (1:6), Tyre (1:9), Edom (1:11), Ammon (1:13), and Moab (2:1). The audience to these indictments could hardly be more pleased. But then in 2:4 and 6 the prophetic ax falls on Judah and Israel, the real objects of Amos' proclamation. The same device appears in the parable of the unjust servant in Matthew 18:23–35. The hearer of the parable witnesses the gross injustice of the unjust servant, morally inexcusable for absolute severity with others when the servant has enjoyed astonishing generosity, and is aroused to righteous indignation. Then dawns the realization that the hearer is in fact the one to whom the parable is directed.[72] The relation of this to classical rhetoric must not be pressed too far, but in the *Poetics of Aristotle* "the most powerful elements of emotional interest in tragedy" are identified as reversal *(peripeteia)* of the situation (or intention) and recognition *(anagnōsis)*.[73] "Thus in the Oedipus, the messenger comes to cheer Oedipus and free him from his alarms about his mother, but by revealing who he is, he produces the opposite effect [*Poetics* XI.1]." That is, a message intended as good news suffers reversal when Oedipus comes to the recognition of who he is.

A number of supportive arguments can now be adduced that reinforce the thesis that in its context Romans 1:26f. serves a dogmatic or rhetorical function, rather than a purpose of moral exhortation (parenesis) deriving from Paul's basic theological outlook.

First, in Bornkamm's discussion of parenesis[74] it is underlined that the list of vices and/or virtues is a characteristic style-form in the New Testament for such parenesis, especially in the letters, in which "for the most part it constitutes their concluding portion." He cites Romans 1:29–31 as an exception to this, but on the terms I have suggested it is not an exception but a confirmation. The parenesis of Romans according to traditional subdivisions of its content begins at Romans 12. This is confirmed by Wilhelm Wuellner's analysis based on rhetorical criticism.[75] By requiring Romans 1:26f.

---

[72]Dan O. Via, *The Parables* (Philadelphia: Fortress Press, 1967), pp. 110–44, has admirably developed the theme of recognition in connection with five parables he designates "tragic."

[73]Aristotle, *Poetics*, ed. and trans. S.H. Butler, 3d ed. (London: Macmillan, 1902), VI.13 (p. 27); XI.1–6 (pp. 41–43).

[74]Günther Bornkamm, "Formen und Gattungen," *Die Religion in Geschichte und Gegenwart*, hrsg. Kurt Galling, 3. Aufl. (Tübingen: J.C.B. Mohr, 1958), 3:1004.

[75]Wilhelm Wuellner, "Paul's Rhetoric of Argumentation in Romans," *Catholic Biblical Quarterly* 38 (1976):345–48.

to serve a parenetic function, its dogmatic and rhetorical intention is circumvented; both the theology and the ethic of Paul are obscured.

Robert Jewett proposes[76] that Romans as a whole be taken as an example of "epideictic" oratory, like that of an ambasssador, which "appeals" (cf. Romans 12:1; 15:30; 16:17) for an affirmative response to some diplomatic objective. This objective, largely but not exclusively, is Paul's favorable reception at Rome as an intermediate destination for prosecuting his westward mission to Spain (1:9–15; 15:24, 28). Pertinent to what I am arguing, Paul must use ideas compatible at points with the recipients' outlook in order to establish a common ground for his appeal. In line with this, Jewett goes on to say of Romans: "More than in any other letter, Paul cites materials that seem alien to his own theology."[77] I maintain— without trying to ascribe this implication to Jewett—that the distance between Paul's *words* in Romans 1:18–32 and his *meaning* or *intention* is critical, decisive. As an analogy, one could point to 1 Corinthians 14:18 ("I thank God that I speak in tongues more than you all"). To assume from this, as some mistakenly do, that 1 Corinthians 12—14 provides a solid Pauline corroboration of glossalalic expression is a stark example of prooftexting myopia.

Second, the proposed interpretation resolves the long debate about the meaning of the conjunction therefore *(dio)* that stands at Romans 2:1. Otto Michel, wrestling with the ancient problem of how a consequential conjunction linking back to the foregoing material (of Romans 1) could make any sense, concluded that *dio* had lost here its original meaning "therefore" and had become a "simple transitional participle."[78] Applying a somewhat characteristic surgical remedy to the problem, Rudolf Bultmann proposed the deletion of 2:1, commending the smooth transition from Romans 1:32 to 2:2.[79] Neither of these remedies is necessary. Anders Nygren had

---

[76] Robert Jewett, "Romans as an Ambassadorial Letter," *Interpretation* 36 (1982): 5–20.

[77] Ibid., p. 19. My reticence about Jewett's hypothesis arises from the unsavory aspect of rhetorical "persuasion" about which Paul is informed. See Hans D. Betz, *Galatians*, Hermeneia (Philadelphia: Fortress Press, 1979), pp. 54–56 on Galatians 1:10. Are we to assume, on Jewett's terms, a shift toward ambiguous speech (cf. 2 Corinthians 1:15–22) in Romans by comparison with the unambiguous quality of Galatians?

[78] Otto Michel, *Der Brief an die Römer,* 4. Aufl., Meyers kritischexegetischer Kommentar über Das Neuen Testament (Göttingen: Vandenhoeck & Ruprecht, 1966), p. 73.

[79] Rudolf Bultmann, "Glossen im Römerbrief," *Theologische Literaturzeitung,* 72 (1947):200.

already noted[80] that the appropriateness of the "therefore" at 2:1 arises from the fact that stereotypical attitudes from the Book of Wisdom looking out in boastful disdain on the lawless goyim provide its rationale. Paul's dark picture of gentile vice is lifted from the mind-set of the one who is already (before the reversal, before the moment of recognition) addressed in chapter 1. So the conjunction in 2:1 simply means: "In face of these condemnations you impose on others, you *therefore* are brought under indictment."

Third, the rhetorical function of Romans 1:18–32 casts important light on the complex issue of whom Paul is addressing in Romans. F.C. Baur's essay on the purpose and occasion of Romans[81] attempted to demonstrate that, as in other epistles, Paul was always preoccupied by the persistent particularism of Jewish Christians who sought to sustain the necessity of legal observances even in the new situation of gentile Christianity. Baur used this conflict as the comprehensive base from which the purpose of Romans should be perceived, and despite numerous corrective efforts against Baur, the insight of his contribution cannot be taken lightly.

Werner G. Kümmel is an example of those who correct Baur. After identifying the Roman readers as predominantly gentile Christians, Kümmel hastens to add that the Roman church "is *not purely Gentile*-Christian."[82] This is an important qualification. But after treating the discussion of the strong and the weak in Romans 14 and 15, along with other concrete polemical elements of the epistle, Kümmel moves even further, saying, "Clearly the crucial point of the letter does not lie in this concrete polemic, but in the exposition of the Pauline message of salvation in constant argument with the Jewish doctrine of salvation."[83] This statement means that the thematic core of Romans cannot be understood outside the parameters of Paul's struggle against legal rectitude as a substitute for Christian liberty. On terms suggested by the rhetorical construction of Romans 1 and 2, it is not necessary to conclude that only Jewish Christians are addressed. In all likelihood we can never know how many members of the Roman congregation were of Jew-

---

[80] Nygren, *Commentary on Romans*, p. 116.

[81] F.C. Baur, "Über Zweck und Veranlassung des Römerbriefs und die damit zusammenhängenden Verhältnisse der römischen Gemeinde," in *Ausgewählte Werke in Einzelausgaben*, Bd. 1, hrsg. v. Klaus Scholder, mit einer Einführung v. E. Käsemann (Stuttgart: Friederich Frommann, 1963), pp. 147–266 (first published in the *Tübinger Zeitschrift für Theologie*, 1836, Heft 3, 59–178).

[82] Kümmel, *Introduction to the New Testament*, p. 310.

[83] Ibid., p. 314.

ish descent and how many were gentile. But we can discern what the burden of Paul's message is: by faith, freedom. This message lies at the foundation of Paul's amazing reconstruction of the *historical* meaning of Habakkuk 2:4 (the righteous one shall live by faithfulness) into the meaning that becomes the theme of Romans at 1:17, the one who through faith (in Jesus) is justified shall live. This theme always preoccupies Paul and explains (polemically) Romans 10:4, "For Christ is the end of the law, that every one who has faith may be justified." Paul's discontinuity with legal rectitude emerges as early as Romans 1:5, in which he speaks of "the obedience of faith." Of this phrase Michel comments: "Obviously, this expression is meant antithetically and polemically," and "Paul stands even here in discussion with Judaism and Jewish Christianity."[84] The same theme breaks out at Romans 1:23, in which Walter Schmithals has correctly discerned the wit that suffuses Paul's putative address on gentile idolatry:

> Paul speaks first of a revelation of God's deity accessible to all people and, in this framework (1:18–21a, 32), discloses the sins of humankind in a manner like that of the pious Jew passing habitual judgment upon the Gentiles. That Paul, however, in no way wishes to exempt the Jews from this judgment is shown by 1:23f: Paul opens the description of the sinful revolt of humanity from God with words from Ps 106:20, which speak of the idolatry of Israel. Precisely *because* the verdict of God rightly falls upon sinners (2:2), the Jews who pass judgment on the heathen also cannot—Ps 106 shows that—elude the divine sentence (2:3–5).[85]

This comment further indicates that Paul takes up the prophetic viewpoint as over against that of Deuteronomic history.

From the standpoint of the cultural criticism of Paul's writings and from the standpoint of the theology of gay/lesbian liberation, the placing of Romans 1:26f. in a rhetorical context forbids the use of that passage for the moral condemnation of homosexuality in itself even if the reader chose to disregard the obvious sense of the text that the persons addressed are "natural" heterosexuals engaging in homosexual acts. There are three objections to the proposed rhetor-

[84] Michel, *Der Brief an die Römer,* pp. 41–42.
[85] Walter Schmithals, *Der Römerbrief als historisches Problem,* Studien zum Neuen Testament 9 (Gütersloh: Gerd Mohn, 1975), p. 13. Cf. also Klaus Berger, *Exegese des Neuen Testaments,* Uni-Taschenbuch 658 (Heidelberg: Quelle & Meyer, 1977), p. 26: "Of course 1:23 refers unmistakably to the golden calf, and the entire passage is to be compared to Naphtali 3—4, where it expressly says of the Jews who can recognize the creator (!) that they will do the evil of the heathen."

ical interpretation of these verses, with which I close this part of the discussion. Two objections are exegetical; the other is moral.

The first objection would appeal to the list of evildoers in 1 Corinthians 6:9–10 as a case in which parenetic use of such a list must be defended. This discussion has not asserted that 1 Corinthians 6:9 is rhetorical or nonparenetic. I do claim, however, that the threefold Levitical tradition (idolatry-adultery-homosexuality) common to 1 Corinthians 6:9f. and Romans 1:18–32 is alien to the spirit of Paul's theology in its discontinuity with the legal rectitude at the bottom of the Holiness Code. I propose that the theology of gay/lesbian liberation, which assumes the naturalness to some people of same-sex orientation and acting, must have a valid theological premise for the correction of Paul's parenesis in the very same manner that liberated Christians must deal in a critical way with Paul's patriarchy. This is not an endorsement of homosexual prostitution or of heterosexual prostitution; nor is it a license for sexual violence or promiscuity.

Another exegetical objection arises from Romans 3:9: "What then? Are we Jews any better off? No, not at all; for I have already charged that all [people], both Jews and Greeks, are under the power of sin." In this text Paul looks back over the earlier part of his discussion, including Romans 1:18–32, and incorporates Greeks under the power of sin. Does this not show that Paul speaks in the last half of Romans 1 in a morally serious way of gentile sin? Paul certainly does not whitewash gentile sin; and nothing that has been said about the rhetorical construction of Romans 1:18ff. is intended to imply that Paul treats Jews severely but pays no attention to gentile wrongdoing. The brunt of my argument is that Paul's preoccupation in Romans throughout is with the inadequacy of legal rectitude. Analogously, the theology of gay/lesbian liberation in no way presumes that confession, absolution, or the means of grace is not applicable to the homosexual. But when access to the means of grace is prefaced by the demand to adopt the culture of heterosexuality, the very meaning of grace itself is reduced to a legal requirement. The moral life from the standpoint of the freedom grace bestows is acting out in freedom, within the multitude of variant circumstances in which we find ourselves, the implications of grace. This is why gay and lesbian Christians who are shut out of the heterosexual church immediately recognize that these churches are like "white" churches that say in attitude and conduct, "Blacks, stay out."

Finally, it might be objected that reemphasis of Paul's historic controversy with legal rectitude in the culture of Judaism will only fuel the fires of anti-Semitism, so that my proposal, like those of F.C. Baur, would falsify Paul's continuity with his rabbinical roots. Liberated Jewish gays and lesbians will indeed have to construct their own theology of gay/lesbian liberation. But this will take place only when historic biblical prohibitions that we have discussed are brought into responsible relationship with contemporary sexology.

In November 1982 the Reform Synagogues of Great Britain issued a pamphlet written by a working party with a number of rabbis on it and led by Dr. Wendy Greengross, a general practitioner and teacher of counseling in North London. The pamphlet asks reform synagogues to accept homosexuals as they are. One rabbi, a member of the working group preparing the document, commented, "Judaism has a particular obligation to embattled minorities."[86]

The biblical expositions of this book are in no sense defamatory of Judaism. The construction of a theology of gay/lesbian liberation must fall on Protestants, Catholics, and Jews alike.

POSTSCRIPT ON 1 TIMOTHY 1:10; JUDE 7; 2 PETER 2:6–8

The two lists of wrongdoers in 1 Corinthians 6:9–10 and 1 Timothy 1:9–10 have in common only *pornoi*, rendered at 1 Timothy 1:10 by the RSV as "immoral persons," and *arsenokoitai* in the same verse that the RSV still renders "sodomites." (This regressive translation should be ᴄmended.) It is important to distinguish between the ethic of the Pastorals (1 and 2 Timothy, Titus) and that of the genuine Pauline epistles.

The author of 1 Timothy closes off the list of wrongdoers with a characteristic reference to "sound doctrine" *(he hygiainousa didaskalia)* as a basic guiding principle. This phrase is not used by Paul in the undisputed epistles. It is a formulary expression referring to a dogmatic standard of orthopraxy that has in time superseded the distinctive liberationist elements of the Pauline gospel, moving closer to rational and moral assumptions of the Stoics. One feels in the Pastorals overall that "the dialectic of the eschatological existence is no longer understood in its original keenness."[87] Not only is the egalitarian vision of Galatians 3:28 left behind, but also Paul's patriarchalism is carried to its ultimate New Testament level in

---

[86] John Whale, "Leviticus Revisited," (London) *Sunday Times*, November 21, 1982.
[87] Martin Dibelius and Hans Conzelmann, *The Pastoral Epistles*, trans. P. Buttolph and A. Yarbro, Hermeneia (Philadelphia: Fortress Press, 1972), p. 41.

1 Timothy 2:11–15, in which deception of Eve (but not Adam) is canonized. In the Pastorals faith is not locked in deadly struggle with works, as in the Pauline epistles, but takes its place alongside other moral virtues (cf. 1 Timothy 2:15; 6:11). This sacrifices the creative centrality of faith, its tension with legal rectitude, and its ability to establish new precedents of moral intuition. Because the Pastorals represent in moral history a trend toward Constantinianism, episcopal "order," and ecclesiastical establishmentarianism, one does not look to them for social pioneering. It is not therefore surprising that some "Bible" churches have found reason in them to bar women from ecclesiastical office (cf. 1 Timothy 2:12; 3:2, 12; Titus 1:6) or, in earlier times, to command the submissiveness of slaves (1 Timothy 6:1–2; Titus 2:9–10). Unless the liberationist elements of Paul's thought are allowed to exercise authority over these cultural accommodations, the bad name that biblical ethics has acquired in times of struggle for human rights will not be altered.

D.S. Bailey has traced the connection between the disobedient angels that "did not keep their own position but left their proper dwelling" (Jude 6) and the waywardness of Sodom and Gomorrah (Jude 7) to a Jewish tradition represented in the pseudepigraphical books of Jubilees 7:20–22 and 20:5–6 and the Testament of Naphtali 3:4–5.[88] The mythology of disobedient angels, watchers, or sons of God, as they are variously called, is based on Genesis 6:1–4, in which, as Jubilees 7:21 expresses the matter, "the Watchers against the law of their ordinances went a-whoring after the daughters of men."[89] This violation of appointed station and general human wickedness occasion the devastating judgment of God expressed in the flood of Genesis 7.

The pivotal phrase in the Sodom (and Gomorrah) reference of Jude 7 is, literally, "going after other flesh" *(apelthousai opisō sarkos heteras)*. Because this stands alongside the angels that violated their appointed status by consorting with the daughters of men in the verse preceding, it is consistent with the context to say that Sodom's offense was likewise the violation of appointed status, although here it is mortals lusting after angels, the reverse of verse 6.

That this is the emphasis intended by Jude is confirmed by the larger context, that is, the attack on false teachers. As M.R. James

[88] D.S. Bailey, *Homosexuality and the Western Christian Tradition* (London: Longmans, Green, 1955), pp. 12–14.

[89] R.H. Charles, *The Apocrypha and Pseudepigrapha of the Old Testament*, vol. 2 of Pseudepigrapha (Oxford: Clarendon Press, 1913), p. 24.

put it, the false teachers are "anarchists," disregarding their status by going against authority (Jude 8).[90] These heretics are accused of licentiousness (2 Peter 2:2, 7, 18; Jude 4, 7, 16). The word can, of course, refer to sexual immorality, but without more specific information, the exact meaning of the writers is left obscure. Bo Reicke correctly warns that "fornication" (RSV, "acted immorally") in Jude 7 may refer, as it often does in the New Testament, to idolatry.[91] The licentiousness of 2 Peter 2:2 may only be a synonym for the bringing in of "destructive heresies" by the false teachers described in 2:1.

Same-sex acts are not named in Jude nor in the parallel in 2 Peter 2 and can only be conjecturally imported into the text on the basis of the Sodom allusion. It must be concluded, therefore, that the RSV rendering "indulged in unnatural lust" at Jude 7, if construed to signify same-sex behavior, unnecessarily slants the phrase translated by Bauer's lexicon as (going) "after other kinds of flesh."[92]

This discussion assumes, of course, that Jude and 2 Peter are both pseudonymous writings, composesd after the close of the apostolic period while seeking to perpetuate the credibility of eyewitness testimony. Because 2 Peter 2 depends on Jude it is of even later date.[93]

---

[90] M.R. James, *The Second Epistle of Peter and the General Epistle of Jude*, Cambridge Greek Testament (Cambridge: Cambridge University Press, 1912), p. 23.

[91] Bo Reicke, *The General Epistles of James, Peter, and Jude*, The Anchor Bible (New York: Doubleday, 1964), p. 199.

[92] Walter Bauer, F.W. Gingrich, and F.W. Danker, *A Greek-English Lexicon of the New Testament*, 2d ed. (Chicago: University of Chicago Press, 1979), p. 743.

[93] Kümmel, *Introduction to the New Testament*, pp. 430–34. Hans Conzelmann und A. Lindemann, *Arbeitsbuch zum Neuen Testament*, 3 Aufl., Uni-Taschenbuch 52 (Tübingen: J.C.B. Mohr, 1977), pp. 311–14.

CHAPTER/FIVE

Liberating Love: Sexuality in Prospect

I now seek to correlate liberation, love, and sexuality in such a way as to face concrete ethical implications of the theology of gay/lesbian liberation and to set these implications in a futuristic time frame. One can begin by recalling that the term love is expressed in New Testament language by a special vocabulary: *agapē* and its derivatives.

The verb *agapan* ("to love") in the Greek Old Testament generally goes back to the Hebrew ᵓ*ahabh*. Repeatedly, ᵓ*ahabh* "signifies the vital impulse of the sexes towards one another,"[1] and yet it can also express God's love for Israel, the sublime, covenantal, elective love at the heart of Hebrew faith. In Hosea, the prophet's love for unfaithful Gomer is an allegory of God's love for unfaithful Israel—an indication of how easily God's love and love between a man and a woman (i.e., marital, sexual love) can use the same vocabulary. Ezekiel, similarly, uses '*ahabh* almost exclusively, in the intensive form *(piel)*, to signify sexual desire.[2] It is important to understand that from the Hebrew side at least, *agapē* can be used as easily in the theological as it can in the sociosexual frame of reference.

Aside from the Greek Old Testament, *agapē* is not widely attested in pre-Christian Greek literature, especially as a noun. It is some-

[1]Gottfried Quell and Ethelbert Stauffer, *agapaō, ktl., Theological Dictionary of the New Testament,* ed. Gerhard Kittel, trans. and ed. G. W. Bromiley (Grand Rapids, MI: Wm. B. Eerdmans, 1968), 1:21. The sexual use of ᵓ*ahabh* is also emphasized by Gerhard Wallis, '*ahabh, Theological Dictionary of the Old Testament,* ed. G. Johannes Botterweck and Helmer Ringgren, trans. J.T. Willis (Grand Rapids, MI: Wm. B. Eerdmans, 1974), 1:107.

[2]Quell and Stauffer, *TDNT,* 1:23.

what imprecise in connotation and is found as a synonym for *erōs* (erotic love) and *philia* (friendship love). Sexual love is pervasively expressed by *erōs* and its derivatives. For example, Kenneth Dover, throughout his study of *Greek Homosexuality*, uses *erastēs* ("lover") and *erōmenos* ("beloved") to discuss partners in sexual love between males. But *erōs* never appears in the New Testament, an omission ascribed by Daniel Day Williams to the probability that "in the Hellenistic period it had acquired a connotation of sensuality and degradation."[3]

Erōs is not simply "erotic" in a sexual sense among the Greeks. In fact, behind the sexual *erōs* lies a larger philosophical signification. Anders Nygren takes *erōs* straight back to Plato's idealism, in his monumental work on *Agape and Eros*.[4] According to this lineage, the soul "remembers" its preexistence in the heavenly world of ideas. When the soul enters time and space, and takes on historical existence, it senses its separation from eternal being. In the body, therefore, the soul is in prison. Its recollection of its eternal, heavenly origin causes the soul to long for its former blissful beautiful abode, as in exile. This longing is precisely *erōs*, "the longing of the soul upwards toward the world of ideas." The desire to have that which is now lacking is obviously egocentric (one of Nygren's favorite characterizations of *erōs*), but the reaching out for the beautiful whether in sexuality or in art is at bottom a reaching upward toward the world of ideas in which true reality rests. The sensual longing may then actually obscure the ideal object of human desire.[5] It is clear from this that *erōs* in Greek thought can signify something other than sexual love and does in some settings conflict with it.

Agapē in the New Testament speaks of the evangelical love of God by which the only, Unique Son of God was sent for human deliverance (John 3:16). The unselfish, sacrificial quality of *agapē* is supremely evidenced in the cross. God's *agapē* toward us was demon-

---

[3] Daniel Day Williams, "Love," in Marvin Halverson and Arthur A. Cohen, eds., *Handbook of Christian Theology* (New York: Meridian, 1958), p. 217.

[4] Anders Nygren, *Agape and Eros*, rev. ed., trans. P.S. Watson (Philadelphia: Westminster Press, 1953), pp. 166–81.

[5] In this context I would locate the famous Alcibiades episode in Plato's *Symposium* 218C–219C, in which Alcibiades arranges to get Socrates in his bed; but Socrates fails to gratify Alcibiades' genital expectations. The story does not mean that Socrates spurns sexual love but can on occasion subordinate it to the beautiful that is above every earthly representation of it.

strated in that while we were yet sinners, without merit, Christ died for us (Romans 5:8).

It is, moreover, clear that the love shown by God is not something wholly other than the love for God and for neighbor that is the cornerstone of New Testament moral instruction (Mark 12:28–33; Matthew 22:34–40; Luke 10:25–37). These injunctions arise from Deuteronomy 6:4–5 and Leviticus 19:18. They employ the verb ʾahabh in the Hebrew. This verb, as noted earlier, frequently expresses sexual love, and whatever the reasons for the avoidance of eran by New Testament writers, agapan from its Hebrew ancestry can apply to connubial love, as shown in Ephesians 5:25, which enjoins the love of husbands and wives.

The love of God for the world becomes in evangelical belief the distinctive element in the formation of all human loves. For example, the statement that God is love (1 John 4:8, 16) is immediately linked by context with interhuman love. "Beloved, let us love one another [1 John 4:7]." "We love, because [God] first loved us [1 John 4:19]." So the advent and dying of God's Son (1 John 4:9–10) is that which informs and transforms human love.

The statement that God is love cannot grammatically or theologically be reversed to read, "Love is God."[6] The future of interhuman love is not in rendering God obsolete by the mature appropriation of God's agapē in human relations. No, human love is carried forward toward its completeness by the sacrificial and suffering love of God, its supreme end and destiny. This does not mean that justice is sentimentalized by love in Johannine belief or that theology minimizes social responsibility. José Miranda has correctly correlated "every one who loves is born of God" in 1 John 4:7 with "every one who does justice is born of God" in 1 John 2:29, showing the synonymous and complementary force of these expressions.[7] The sociological setting of the assertion that God is love is sustained and climaxed at the end of 1 John 4, where the one saying, "I love God," but hating brother or sister is designated a liar (1 John 4:20–21).

It is true that interhuman love in 1 John 4 does not explicitly

[6] Rudolf Bultmann, The Johannine Epistles, trans. R. P. O'Hara and others, Hermeneia (Philadelphia: Fortress Press, 1973), p. 66.
[7] José Miranda, Being and the Messiah: The Message of St. John, trans. John Eagelson (Maryknoll, NY: Orbis Books, 1977), pp. 71–90.

name sexual love. Implicit in the love commandment, however, is the unquestionable task of carrying it forward into the total arena of human experience. Repeatedly and patriarchally, 1 John enjoins the love of brother (2:9, 10, 11; 3:10, 14, 15, 16, 17; 4:20, 21).[8] Unless Christian morality is to be locked up in the first century and its future thereby abandoned, the criticism of patriarchy inherent in *agapē* itself must be exercised. Nygren's analysis of *agapē* and *erōs* contains many remarkable insights that continue to enrich human knowledge. However, the systematic polarization of erotic love on the one hand as egocentric and self-fulfilling and agapeic love on the other hand as sacrificial and self-giving, has the net result of placing a moral ban on sexual love.[9] If this tendency toward a radical dichotomy between *erōs* and *agapē* is linked with a moral indifference to New Testament masculinity, the transforming power of *agapē* not only within human sexuality but also within civilization generally is seriously abridged.

A summary statement about the liberative quality of *agapē* is also necessary. In the same degree that Paul understands legal rectitude as bondage, to the same degree is the love of God at work for liberation. The "custodian" (Greek, *paidagōgos*) of Galatians 3:23–29 should not be understood as serving the role of a benevolent supervisor.[10] The law in this passage is not an intermediate step in human evolution toward completeness but a confinement that summons to liberation. That is the reason the guardian stands in context with the broken bondage of race, class, and sex proclaimed in Galatians 3:28 as the consequence of baptism. The climax of Paul's freedom affirmation contained in Romans 5—8[11] is in Romans 8:31–39, often cited as the apex of Paul's theological insight. The depths of mortal trial come to expression in this passage. These appear in the concrete experiences (vss. 35–36) that link Paul's view of discipleship (cf. 1 Corinthians 4:9–13; 15:30–31; 2 Corinthians 4:7–18, etc.)

[8] Twice in 1 John 2:12–14 appears the poetic sequence, "little children, . . . fathers, . . . young men." Where have all the women gone?

[9] See Daniel Day Williams, *The Spirit and the Forms of Love* (New York: Harper & Row, 1968), pp. 2, 38, 46, 52, 79, 87, 120–21, 128, 208, for various criticisms of Nygren's thesis and method.

[10] Hans D. Betz, *Galatians*, Hermeneia (Philadelphia: Fortress Press, 1979), pp. 177–78.

[11] Anders Nygren, *Commentary on Romans*, trans. Carl C. Rasmussen (Philadelphia: Muhlenberg Press, 1949), pp. 32–35, 191–349, in a widely emulated manner has developed this section as freedom from wrath, sin, law, and death.

with the via crucis. The trial is set by Paul in a cosmic and mythological framework of adversity (vss. 38f. angels, . . . principalities, . . . powers, . . . height, . . . depth) associated with the world view of gnosticism and its grim perception of human bondage.[12] It is the love of Christ (vs. 35; some texts read "love of God") that opposes on our behalf these earthly and supernatural adversaries and empowers the one who knows the love of Christ (vs. 37; cf. Galatians 2:20) in the conquest of them.

From these observations we can now formulate the thesis that occupies us at this point and that will be pursued in the pages following: *Agapē* love morally informs human sexuality and mediates to it the experience of liberation. To express this in an alternative manner, New Testament soteriology is appropriately expressed as liberation, a liberation based on the sacrificial love of God and shaping human relationships, including sexual ones, according to the spirit of this love.

LIBERATING LOVE IN 1 CORINTHIANS 12—14

The whole of 1 and 2 Corinthians can be meaningfully comprehended with the aid of liberationist language. Paul sets forth the theology of redemption through Christ crucified (1 Corinthians 2:2), but he propounds this correctively in face of a Corinthian misperception of the remedy for human oppression. The Corinthian community aspires to freedom and appropriates the sacraments in such a way as to guarantee the believers' translation into a brave new world of heavenly release from the agonies of historical existence. Ernst Käsemann describes the misguided freedom at Corinth like this:

> The disorder at eucharistic celebrations did not come about through any lack of regard for the eucharist in the setting of a love feast; on the contrary, the Lord's Supper was celebrated as an anticipation of the heavenly banquet amid eschatological rejoicing and ecstatic manifestations such as, perhaps, speaking in tongues. It was a demonstration of what was taught in Ephesians 1. This church knew itself to be already

[12]On the function of Gnostic language in Paul, see Rudolf Bultmann, *Theology of the New Testament*, vol. 1, trans. K. Grobel (New York: Macmillan, 1952), pp. 164–83 (on Gnostic Motifs), 230–31, 258–59. Of course, Bultmann existentializes the bondage/liberation axis, but "powers" suggest social and political correlatives as well as subjective ones.

redeemed "in the heavenly places," filled with divine powers, open to the permanent invasion of the earthly by the eternal, and itself testifying to this through its behaviour. The same is true of baptism, which, as we know from 1:10ff., was made an occasion of party divisions. For the baptized people split into different groups according to the master who had baptized them or by whose name a particular group was designated.[13]

While Walter Schmithals' *Gnosticism in Corinth*[14] has been felt by Hans Conzelmann and other students of the Corinthian correspondence to go too far in finding at Corinth a full-blown Gnostic Christology, a wide agreement is found regarding the Corinthian problem as stated by Käsemann. Werner G. Kümmel can, therefore, say that the whole of 1 Corinthians "manifests a front against a Gnostic perversion of the Christian message which attributes to the pneumatics, as those liberated from the *sarx* [flesh], a perfect redemptive state and an unconditional moral freedom."[15]

The unit consisting of 1 Corinthians 12—14 is held together by the theme of charismatic gifts. Paul's own message of liberation has featured the Spirit as the agent of empowerment against human captivity. This is repeatedly shown in Romans 8, in which the Spirit frees from the law of sin and death (8:2), bestows life over against death (8:5–11), effects the adoption of the homeless (8:12–17), and strengthens against infirmity the one who prays (8:26–27). This same Spirit sheds abroad in human hearts the love of God (Romans 5:5). All these images lend themselves to liberationist soteriology and could be used by enthusiasts (etymologically, those "in God") at Corinth for their own egocentric purposes. As shown by 1 Corinthians 7:1; 7:25; 8:1; 12:1; 16:1, Paul takes up subjects about which the church has written to him (7:1). Because 1 Corinthians 14 resumes the discussion of corporate worship vis-à-vis the charismatic phenomena, returning to the ecstatic speaking already broached at 12:11, 28, and 30, the connection between chapters 12 and 14 is clear.

Although Conzelmann finds 1 Corinthians 13 a self-contained unit, with weak linkage at the end of chapter 12 and the beginning

---

[13]Ernst Käsemann, *Jesus Means Freedom*, trans. Frank Clarke (Philadelphia: Fortress Press, 1969), p. 62.

[14]Trans. John E. Steeley (Nashville: Abingdon Press, 1971).

[15]Werner G. Kümmel, *Introduction to the New Testament*, rev. ed., trans. Howard C. Kee (Nashville: Abingdon Press, 1975), p. 274.

of chapter 13,[16] a number of his comments on chapter 13 find their pertinence by reference to chapters 12 and 14; there is no general dispute about the Pauline authorship of chapter 13. On the strength of the canonical position of chapter 13, the absence of manuscript evidence to the contrary, and its significance for the theology of liberating love, the unity of chapters 12—14 is assumed. Johannes Weiss's proposal to place the thirteenth chapter after the fourteenth would not compromise what I want to say about it. Perhaps Paul wrote the *agapē* hymn of chapter 13 separately and subsequently wove it into the present setting with seams still at points visible.

The corrective function chapter 13 serves with respect to Corinthian pneumaticism is unmistakable. The body image of 1 Corinthians 12:12–31 is contextually informed by the message of *agapē*. This image is pre-Christian and first appears in Roman literature (Livy, *Ab Urbe Condita* 2.32) in conjunction with the body politic.[17] In the Christian adaptation of the image the new element is the predicate "of Christ" (12:27). This already shows that the solidarity of the church lies under other auspices than a human awareness of interdependence. Käsemann has strongly argued, on the basis of 12:12–13 (especially the phrase "so it is with Christ"), that what is meant here is not that the church is *like* a body but that it *is* the body of Christ.[18] Since elsewhere (especially, for example, at 2:2) Paul deals polemically with Corinthian misperception of liberation by counterposing Christ crucified, it is once again the theologia crucis, the love of Christ as manifested in his suffering, that rebukes the Corinthian dismemberment.

Conzelmann grants in respect to 1 Corinthians 14:20 (the rebuke of immaturity) that "one can read between the lines that Paul is indirectly characterizing the activities at Corinth as childish."[19] But this statement should also be extended to 13:11. It is true that nowhere in chapters 12—14 does Paul repudiate glossalalia in toto (cf. 14:5, 6, and especially vs. 18), but he curbs it in such a way that

---

[16] Hans Conzelmann, *1 Corinthians*, trans. James W. Leitch and ed. George M. MacRae, Hermeneia (Philadelphia: Fortress Press, 1975), p. 217. Schmithals, *Gnosticism in Corinth*, p. 95, makes similar comments with special reference to Johannes Weiss' relocation of chapter 13 after chapter 14.

[17] References in Conzelmann, *1 Corinthians*, p. 211, n. 7.

[18] Ernst Käsemann, *Perspectives on Paul*, trans. Margaret Kohl (Philadelphia: Fortress Press, 1971), pp. 104, 117. Käsemann first expounded these ideas in *Leib und Leib Christi: Eine Untersuchung zur paulinischen Begrifflichkeit*, Beiträge zur historischen Theologie (Tübingen: J.C.B. Mohr, 1933).

[19] Conzelmann, *1 Corinthians*, p. 241.

the contrast between 14:18 and 14:19 is a virtual contradiction. Conzelmann perceives that in 13:2 Paul follows the Corinthian order of merit (tongues . . . prophecy) but reverses this in 14:1–2, 3–4, 5–6, and so on (prophecy . . . tongues).[20] This is also applicable to chapter 12, in which the list of charismata is given three times (12:8–10, 28, 29–30). In each of these cases, ecstatic utterance (plus its necessary adjunct, interpretation, at the end of vss. 10 and 30) comes at the bottom of the list. The priorities of the Corinthians are therefore consistently reversed in all three chapters.

The fourteenth chapter of 1 Corinthians is held together by the urgency of "edification" (Greek, *oikodomē, oikodomein*), which is explicit at least seven times in the course of the chapter and implicit throughout. If the centerpiece of chapter 12 is integration (on the basis of the body of Christ that is broken), the centerpiece of chapter 14 is edification, and both of these themes are grounded in the *agapē* of chapter 13. And why is prophetic edification valued above speaking in tongues? The latter is self-directed, a private indulgence of religious ecstasy; the former benefits the community (14:4) or even outsiders (14:23–25).

Social concern on the basis of *agapē*, therefore, constitutes a transvaluation of the Corinthian valuation that wrongly considers the degree of unintelligibility in ecstatic outburst a proportionate "indication of the working of supernatural power."[21] Hence it is impossible to mistake the reasoning that underlies the word of the cross (1 Corinthians 1:18) as the cornerstone of the Corinthian correspondence. Christ crucified (2:2) is not only that which determines the cruciform character of the apostolic ministry (4:9–13), but also that which undermines the self-seeking triumphalism at Corinth (4:6–8) and its drift into chauvinistic disintegration (1:10–17; chapter 3; cf. "puffed up" at 4:6, 18, 19; 5:2; 8:1; 13:4).

This same perspective informs the problem of sexuality at Corinth. Just as Paul does not condemn glossalalia as such, or even gnosis (counted at 1:5 as an enrichment), his treatment of sexuality is controlled by an awareness of its abuses and the necessity of ordering its manifestations under the transvaluation inherent in *agapē*. The instances of incest and fornication at 1 Corinthians 5 should be considered in the same way. Gnostic dualism attempted to place the person beyond the flesh *(sarx)* into the world of the

[20] Ibid., p. 222.
[21] Ibid., pp. 233f.

spirit *(pneuma)*. By virtue of this liberation into pneumatic, heavenly existence, sexuality could be uninhibitedly exercised (because the pneumatic was already beyond the reality of flesh) or (for the same reason) a complete renunciation of sex could be practiced. The former course was probably more popular than the latter.

Paul's remedy for uninhibited sexual freedom is terse: flee fornication (6:18). But as R.H. Fuller comments: "His answer to asceticism is not so satisfactory."[22] Chapter 7 of 1 Corinthians, to which Fuller's comments on Corinthian asceticism are directed, does not lend itself to intelligible exegesis without appeal to 1 Corinthians 13. On the one hand, Paul seems to approve sexual abstinence (7:1, 8, 27, 32, 34), but he counters his own approval of it by a concession in each case to the sexual drive (7:2–6, 9, 28, 36–39). The chapter is also overshadowed by an apocalyptic expectation underlying 7:29 and 31, an expectation that after nineteen centuries shows itself untenable in the form Paul seems to have conceived it.

The fact that Paul's discussion of sexuality is overshadowed by a vision of the End strongly suggests the relation in which sexuality stands to *agapē*. Sexual love is paradoxical in its ability to express self-centered, instinctive, and immediate gratification, on the one hand, and powerful self-giving on the other.[23] The moral task of theology is to exemplify and teach the fulfilling of sexual love in self-giving *agapē*. This *agapē* is the basis for a mutuality that no longer seeks surrender and self-sacrifice from the other, pleasure and domination for the self.

Despite Paul's apostleship to the gentiles and misguided Gnostic freedom at Corinth, it is improbable that he could forget the sexual use of Hebrew *'ahabh (agapan)*[24] in the richly sensual way it appears in the Song of Songs or that use of it in Hosea 11:1 to describe a love of God that eventuates in the Exodus. Daniel Day Williams strongly emphasizes the experience of sexuality in terms of process, an event in the pilgrimage of the self, especially as we exercise the measure of freedom that is always present in deciding how we shall live in a sexual way.[25] There is a profound sense in which neighbor

[22] R.H. Fuller, *A Critical Introduction to the New Testament* (London: Duckworth, 1966), p. 44.

[23] Williams, *The Spirit and the Forms of Love*, p. 214. Williams' entire discussion of love and sexuality (pp. 214–42) has greatly aided my understanding at this point.

[24] Eighteen instances of *'ahabh* (noun or verb) are translated by *agapē/agapan* in the Septuagint version of the Song of Songs.

[25] Williams, *The Spirit and the Forms of Love*, pp. 225–26.

love (Leviticus 19:18; Mark 12:31; Matthew 22:39; Luke 10:27–37) marks the future toward which sexual love moves to fulfillment and gives to sexual love its moral depth. As Williams put this:

> The need for the love which gives faithfulness to the other, suffers with and for the other, and accepts the other, pervades the whole sexual experience. We say the need for *agapē* because we are often far from realizing or accepting its presence. It can make itself known as need long before we know its creative and healing power.[26]

The final section of 1 Corinthians 13 (vss. 8–13) extols the constancy of *agapē* against the transience of the charismata (prophecy, tongues, gnosis). The last two, at least, have commanded the loyalty of the Corinthian church under the impression that they are the ultimate signs of human deliverance. In 13:8 *agapē* does not have the character of another charisma in addition to those listed. This is also the case in 13:1–3. Again, in 14:1, *agapē* is of another order of being than the spiritual gifts. The result of this distinction is that *agapē* exists alongside or through the charismata and arranges them according to the respective functions they serve in the economy of human liberation. The theme of the discussion can now be restated. Sexuality is a gift of God, a medium of ecstatic power pointing beyond itself to the love of God manifested in the suffering of Christ. The *agapē* of God delivers sexuality from a false autonomy destined for futility and orders it according to the total task of that freedom it is summoned to serve.

SEXUALITY IN PROSPECT: AN ETHICAL PROFILE

Daniel Day Williams published his work on *The Spirit and the Forms of Love,* with its insightful correlation of *agapē* and sexuality, in 1968. This was a year earlier than the Stonewall rebellion of June 28, 1969, termed by Dennis Altman "The Boston Tea Party" of the gay/lesbian movement.[27] The Stonewall Inn was a dance bar on Christopher Street in New York City. On that night there was a police raid for alleged infringement of liquor laws, not an uncommon occurrence among establishments serving homosexual patrons. The difference on this occasion was that the patrons fought

---

[26] Ibid., p. 231.
[27] Dennis Altman, *Homosexual Oppression and Liberation* (New York: Avon Books, 1971), p. 117.

back. The police found themselves barricaded inside the bar while it was pelted by bottles, cans, and brickbats. Following the three-day disturbance at Christopher Street, the Gay Liberation Front (GLF) was organized and began publishing its newspaper, *Come Out!* In the fall of 1970 the GLF was organized in London by Aubrey Walter and Bob Mellors, and by early 1971 the weekly meetings (at All Saints' Parish Hall, Notting Hill Gate) were numbering four to five hundred people.[28] The newspaper of the London GLF was called *Come Together!*

Williams' 1968 discussion of sexuality and *agapē* does not include homosexuality, but the assumption of this treatment of the future of sexuality is that the relation of homosexuality to *agapē* is no different in principle than that of heterosexuality. Indeed, in that gay and lesbian persons sense in a special way the politics of repression, they have a particular potentiality for perceiving the original sense in which the liberating love of God manifests itself on the human scene. So what is said about sexuality in prospect and the ethical themes selected to represent it are intended no more for one than the other orientation whatever examples are introduced.

1. *Constancy* is a primary measure of sexual liberation that is brought under the jurisdiction of *agapē*. This emerges from the fact that *agapē* endures after the moments of human ecstasy that ignite our consciences and set us on our way have passed. Jeffrey Weeks writes as a friend and advocate of gay/lesbian liberation, but after assessing the inner divisions—fragmentation began at Corinth with baptism (1 Corinthians 1:10–17)—that appeared in the movement by the end of the first year, he could write with some sadness: "GLF was vulnerable to the change of climate. It had been the last major product of late 1960s euphoria; it collapsed as that euphoria died. It had already exhausted itself in the United States by 1971, and events in such other major capitalist countries as Australia were to follow a similar pattern."[29]

It would be as erroneous to assert that gay/lesbian liberation ended in 1971 as it would be to think that it began only on June 28, 1969, on Christopher Street, New York City. Constancy not only embraces the hope that goes on beyond the passing of particular organizations that play a prominent role at a given moment in the

[28] Jeffrey Weeks, *Coming Out* (New York: Quartet, 1977), pp. 188–89.
[29] Ibid., p. 206.

shaping of new cultural possibilities, but it also recognizes the seeds sown in times long forgotten by those who struggled in unsung solitude for the end of sexual oppression. Constancy in this sense links us to the history of human freedom before and after the time of our attention to it.

Williams treats constancy in another ethically significant sense. Writing of heterosexual love from the standpoint of process thought, he was moved in the 1960s by the cultural forces that associated sexual liberation with instant sexual intimacy and the repudiation of moral prescriptions associated with the Judeo-Christian tradition of monogamy.

In this context it is appropriate to recall the liberationist understanding of the monogamy precept in Mark 10:2–12.[30] That is, the proscription of divorce in the Marcan tradition is set against the male trivialization of the Mosaic permission of divorce in Deuteronomy 24:1–4, a trivialization that could only victimize the woman on the basis of the sexual whims of the husband. It is further clear that the Marcan divorce pericope, although directed against divorce for the defense of female rights, must already cope with the factual occurrence of divorce in the community. In fact, the right of the woman to initiate divorce is implied in Mark 10:12 and represents in its own way a Roman extension of the liberationist intent of the original Palestinian prescription.

Williams recognizes that the legal fulfillment of a monogamous contract in which "growth in freedom and love" does not manifest itself is not a case of responsiveness to *agapē;* so divorce cannot be ruled out, and laws against it imposed by the zeal of religious communities are contrary to the well-being of democratic societies.[31] Therefore, I find Williams' reflections as a "soft monogamist" to be a valid statement of one aspect of constancy as a moral measure of the liberation of human sexuality. It is difficult to believe that continued erosion of the monogamous culture can have any other result in the patriarchal situation, however, than the reinforcement of female oppression.

Williams does not appeal for sexual constancy on the basis of a deontological biblical legalism, that is, a heavy emphasis on the

[30] The exception clause placed in the Matthaean redaction at Matthew 5:32 and 19:9 shows further accommodation to the fact of early Christian divorce, although Matthew's masculinity stands out also.

[31] Williams, *The Spirit and the Forms of Love,* pp. 237–38.

moral "oughtness" of specific biblical commandments without consideration of the historical context, both ancient and contemporary, in which such commandments arose and are to be applied. His discerning correlation of *erōs* and *agapē* arises from his vision that the goal of *agapē* is communion, companionship, and reconciliation.[32] This is the quality of *agapē* that emerges in Paul's affirmation, against a powerful array of anguishing experiences to the contrary, that nothing can "separate us from the love of God [Rom. 8:39]."

It is the constancy of the love of God shown in Christ that gives to human love—including sexual love—its quality as history[33] in which sexuality becomes a renewal of the acceptance of another and "the willingness to be transformed for the sake of the other." To withhold one's self from this interchange with the other at the deeper level, even at the level of sacrifice, deprives sexuality of its liberative power and allows it, cut off from constancy, to assume, unopposed, an ephemeral episodic quality deprived of its future. Too many people are denied in this way the joy of growing old together in love.

Constancy undermines promiscuity and cannot be reconciled with it. On premises removed from moral and religious reflection in the explicit sense, Alan P. Bell and Martin S. Weinberg, William Masters and Virginia Johnson, and others whose work provides opportunity for wide observation of sexual habits and mores have emphasized that constancy among some homosexuals is well attested despite the absence of "liturgical support of gay unions" described by James Nelson as obligatory if the church is not to be caught in "a humanly destructive contradiction" of condemning homosexual relationships for inconstancy while doing nothing to encourage its opposite.[34]

Norman Pittenger finds that homosexual acts, just as those heterosexual, are capable of expressing "the movement of persons toward mutual fulfilment and fulfilment in mutuality, with all the accompanying characteristics of love."[35] This leads Pittenger to the valuing of commitment and the disapproval of promiscuity.

[32] Ibid., p. 14.
[33] Ibid., p. 228.
[34] James Nelson, "Gayness and Homosexuality: Issues for the Church," in *Homosexuality and Ethics*, ed. Edward Batchelor, Jr. (New York: Pilgrim Press, 1980), p. 209.
[35] Norman Pittenger, "The Morality of Homosexual Acts," in *Homosexuality and Ethics*, ed. Batchelor, Jr., p. 141.

Since, however, heterosexual love is beset with so much inconstancy in our time, Pittenger warns also against the double standard. He points out the importance of pastoral counseling aimed at aiding gay or lesbian couples to resolve the problems that jeopardize ongoing and growing relationship. In repeated instances Masters and Johnson discovered in their work that homosexual couples were denied professional counseling services for sexual dysfunction, despite their request for such help.

At the same time it is illogical for homosexuals to lay the total blame for promiscuity at the door of the homophobic society. If the absence of supportive social mandates, customs, and rituals were the only determinant of inconstancy in homosexual relations, the absence of such constancy in heterosexual relations that have full access to these mandates, customs, and rituals cannot be explained. If, furthermore, human beings have no control, no discretionary judgment in the exercise of sexuality, it is useless to discuss morality, and liberation itself is a delusion, because we remain totally subject to the sexual drive and its instinctual requirements of the moment.

According to Dennis Altman, Gore Vidal has asserted that "it is possible to have a mature sexual relationship with a woman on Monday, and a mature sexual relationship with a man on Tuesday, and perhaps on Wednesday have both together."[36] It is difficult for me to know when Vidal is not joking. "Mature" also has various definitions, including the use "mature fruit," which means that soon it may begin to stink. The Marquis de Sade wrote for effect, and it is an error for people to take his sexual surrealism too seriously.[37] The humor of sex should not be eclipsed, even in a moral discussion of it. But the bisexuality Vidal propounds in this statement is particularly difficult for the objective of constancy to accommodate. Altman uses the quotation to affirm that "one would expect a liberated society to regard bisexuality as the norm," although he too refuses to take the statement of Vidal as illustrative of what Altman means by bisexuality.[38]

Constancy does impose a particular, perhaps unequal, burden on

---

[36] Altman, *Homosexual Oppression and Liberation*, p. 105.
[37] Herant A. Katchadourian and Donald T. Lunde, *Fundamentals of Human Sexuality*, 2d ed. (New York: Holt, Rinehart & Winston, 1975), p. 455.
[38] Altman, *Homosexual Oppression and Liberation*, p. 105.

those who fall near the center of Kinsey's zero-to-six scale of sexual orientation. Charles Laughton remained in a heterosexual marriage during a successful career in theater and cinema. Oscar Wilde also had a wife and children. Sappho too was a wife and mother.[39] At a distance it is impossible to know the "history" and quality of that love which is experienced by homosexual people in marriage contracts with those of the opposite sex. Conceivably a genuine mutuality and growth in freedom exists in circumstances that would not seem conducive to it. But such a possibility does not overrule the likelihood that contracts entered into with the hope that one's homosexuality or bisexuality would be remedied by marital love, or contracts knowingly entered into in the naive hope that the partner's orientation can—with effort—be reversed, or contracts concluded without candid discussion of one's sexual orientation and intentions could only expect to end in disillusionment.

In Greek society, homosexual love and heterosexual love existed side by side. Famous people like Socrates, as well as ordinary ones, engaged in both. It is sometimes felt that a return to this "bisexual" society is the final stage of liberation from the antisexual repressions of moralistic religion. This point of view is not able to explain, however, the gross abuses of sexual slavery, male and female prostitution (both homo- and heterosexual), or the added consequences of androcentric tyranny in such arrangements of this idyllic past.

Michael Lynch has given a moving account of the relationship between his New York friend, Fred, and Fred's lover, Bruce, after Fred falls victim to Kaposi's Sarcoma, or what is now more inclusively called acquired immunity deficiency syndrome (AIDS).[40] Lynch sees the appearance of AIDS among homosexual males in 1981 as a nightmare comparable to the Dade County, Florida, crusade against homosexual rights in 1977.

Lynch narrates how Fred is told by his physician, after the removal of two small cysts from his ears, that he is infected with Kaposi's sarcoma and will have to undergo chemotherapy. Information on the high mortality of the disease among homosexuals had been published in *The New York Times,* July 3, 1981. Fred and Bruce recognize the seriousness of Fred's condition. Their fears are

[39]C.M. Bowra, "Sappho," in *Oxford Classical Dictionary,* 2d ed., ed. N.G.L. Hammond and H.H. Sculland (Oxford: Clarendon Press, 1970), p. 950.

[40]Michael Lynch, "Living with Kaposi's," *Body Politic* 88 (November 1982):31–37.

accented by effects of the chemotherapy (gross fatigue, hair loss, depression, weight loss). There is a related bout with pneumocystic pneumonia requiring hospitalization and painful daily leg injections.

The heart of the story emerges in the loyalty of Bruce, the deepening bond between Fred and his parents, who sustain their love for him in the crisis of his illness and suffering and also come to accept and appreciate the depth of Bruce's bond to their son. Another friend enters the deepening circle of mutual support between Fred, Bruce, and Fred's parents. These five people become a source of strength to one another, drawn together through pain and resisting the terror death always tends to provoke. Themes of the story unerringly point to liberating love and the suffering through which commitment in love flows healingly over the wounds of mortality. In such trial, people grow. They sort out what is real.

The story should end there, but Lynch uses the record of these loyal people, drawn together in love, to attack the medical profession for preying on gay fears. At the time of Lynch's article no success had been attained in isolating the infectious agent or developing an immunization vaccine for AIDS. The Center for Disease Control in Atlanta had, however, confirmed that three-fourths of the victims were gay or bisexual males among whom frequency of sexual contacts exceeded that of most gay men.[41] In the face of the available information, physicians had begun to caution against promiscuous sexual contacts. Outraged at the "medical model" that he associates with the repressive, moral-medical right wing, Lynch staunchly hails the greatness of promiscuity:

> Since 1969, the post-Stonewall gay movement has unrelentingly scrutinized the medical model and largely rejected all medical definitions of gay people. In the place of these alien labellings, it has burst forward with acts of self-definition, moving well beyond characterizations related to sexual acts ("we are only what we do in bed") but maintaining that sexual brotherhood of promiscuity as the foundation of our identity.[42]

[41] Bill Lewis, "The Real Gay Epidemic: Panic and Paranoia," *Body Politic* 88 (November 1982):40. Lewis is assistant professor of surgery and microbiology at the University of Toronto.

[42] Lynch, "Living with Kaposi's," p. 35. Lynch's view seems close to that of John Rechy in his vigorous reaction to the report of Jonathan Lieberson ("Anatomy of an Epidemic" *New York Review of Books* 30 (August 18, 1983):17–22) on 1983 books treating AIDS. See John Rechy and Jonathan Lieberson, "An Exchange on AIDS," *New York Review of Books* 30 (October 13, 1983):43–45.

I find this glorification of promiscuity, on health grounds alone, grotesque and in itself a wholesale disregard of the steadfast caring that *agapē* implies. Nor do I believe that the majority of those homosexual males who had access to the medical information about AIDS then current would have taken Lynch seriously.

2. *Nonviolence* is a second comprehensive canon of the liberative power of love and the prospect of human sexuality. Appropriately, in the 1963 publication by British Friends, *Towards a Quaker View of Sex*, this criterion occupies an important place: "But first of all any element of force or coercion, or abuse of some superior position must put an act beyond the pale and leave it to be condemned."[43] Obviously, the rejection of "force or coercion, or abuse of some superior position" applies to both hetero- and homosexual acts. The number of women raped, the number of battered wives and of female children sexually abused by fathers, stepfathers, or other men of the house shows how impossible it is to link homosexuality with violence in any manner not widely illustrated in heterosexual relations. "Queer bashing" is one of the historic means of homosexual repression. My first encounter with it some forty years ago prompted reflections on sexuality and violence that still prod my search for ethical sanity.

The episode took place when I worked at the Eastern State Hospital in Williamsburg, Virginia. Ward 5 was the most disturbed of all the wards. It occupied the second floor of an ancient stone and cement building strongly resembling a prison. It was not unusual, even on Ward 5, to be the sole attendant for sixty or seventy male patients. Understaffed and underfunded, the hospital was a vivid example of what liberation writers would call institutional violence, although with a slightly altered meaning.

One summer afternoon I was summoned excitedly from the front of the ward because "somebody was gettin' mauled." I ran down the hall to the back porch, which was enclosed with heavy mesh wire from floor to ceiling. I discovered that a relatively new patient, John, who was muscular, stocky, and about forty, had pushed an older man, Cecil, onto a wooden bench against the inner wall of the porch. Cecil's left leg below the knee was a wooden "peg"—symbol

---

[43] Alastair Heron, "Towards a Christian View of Sex," in Batchelor, ed., *Homosexuality and Ethics*, p. 137. In this publication, the Friends once again stand in the vanguard of Christian moral insight.

of a time predating the amenities of modern prosthetics. John's fists, like a pile driver, were smashing Cecil's face, now unrecognizably marred. Already beaten nearly into unconsciousness, Cecil's head was whipped back and forth in helpless recoil with each smashing blow. Eyebrows and lips were lacerated, bleeding profusely. I screamed John's name, angrily pushing him away from the older man, demanding a reason for his brutal conduct. "Because," he screamed back, "he's a goddamned queer!" John had unexpectedly come across Cecil in an act of fellatio with another male patient.

In July 1982 the Task Force on Gay/Lesbian Issues of the Commission on Social Justice in the Archdiocese of San Francisco completed its report on *Homosexuality and Social Justice.*[44] This report, with its roster of fifty-four recommendations, is addressed throughout to the fact that violence against homosexuals, often lethal violence, had increased markedly in the two years before the report. A random selection of items in the report includes the following:

- A gay male from Seattle stabbed to death on a San Francisco street and his companion wounded by an attacker who first asked if the victims were gay.
- A man attacked by two assailants wielding an iron pipe, on his way home from a gay bar; one eye knocked out, extensive facial injuries.
- A young man mistakenly knifed to death by someone believing him to be homosexual.
- Investigative committee appointed ("Community United Against Violence"—CUAV) by Mayor Dianne Feinstein in 1981, outraged by such assaults. In a single quarterly report, December 31, 1981, CUAV cites more than 100 cases of assault against people of gay/lesbian orientation.
- Acts of violence encouraged by scurrilous propaganda circulated by committees of fundamentalist preachers, the Moral Majority, the antihomosexual "Save Our Souls" Crusade, and a group calling itself "Agape, Inc." (sic).

[44] Published by the Commission on Social Justice, Archdiocese of San Francisco, 441 Church Street, San Francisco, CA 94114. The Task Force chair was Kevin Gordon, a psychotherapist. The report was briefly reviewed in *Time*, October 11, 1982, p. 67.

- The church encouraging denigration of lesbians and gays by neglecting to preach and educate against violent acts of the sort mentioned and patronizing dogmas or policies of denigration.
- An increase by 400 percent in violence against gay/lesbian people after a CBS Report, "Gay Power, Gay Politics," April 26, 1980.

Although the Task Force report is not an official statement of the archdiocese, it was, nevertheless, received as a working document of the Commission on Social Justice.

Dom Helder Camara, Archbishop of Recife, has spoken of the three forms of violence, each provoking the other, as follows: the violence of injustice, the violence of revolution, the violence of repression.[45] Liberation movements arise as a natural consequence of systemic injustice. The task of education is to facilitate the correction of injustice so that the violence of revolution becomes unnecessary. Where this purpose of education is not served, the covert violence of injustice is disregarded, revolution is provoked, and repressive violence sets in.

Accordingly, then, the report on *Homosexuality and Social Justice* is deeply concerned about the covert, systemic violence perpetrated for centuries against homosexual people. The surprising fact is that the gay/lesbian liberation movement, despite marches and demonstrations to raise public awareness about the widespread moral, psychological, and physical violence inflicted by the sexual majority, has not, in general, adopted attitudes of retaliatory violence. This is particularly noteworthy in view of the slow pace of change in public moral attitudes and in the political-legislative process through which repressive laws are changed.

In 1957 the Committee on Homosexual Offenses and Prostitution, appointed by the British Parliament and chaired by Sir John Wolfenden, presented its report after deliberating for three years, holding sixty-two sessions, and hearing more than two hundred witnesses. With reference to homosexuality, the crux of the report was the repeal of a nineteenth-century law making private homosexual acts between consenting adults a criminal offense. The recommended repeal was debated and voted down in May of 1960. In 1965 it passed the House of Lords by a vote of ninety-four to forty-nine. Voting in favor of the repeal was the Marquess of Queens-

[45] Cited by Robert McAfee Brown, *Making Peace in the Global Village* (Philadelphia: Westminster Press, 1981), pp. 28–29.

berry, great grandson of the man who successfully prosecuted Oscar Wilde, sentenced to prison for two years. The repeal was voted down, however, in the House of Commons by nineteen votes. Finally, it was passed by both Houses in July 1967, ten years after the completion of the committee's report.[46]

Legislative remedies in the United States have been even slower in coming. More than half the states still maintain archaic sodomy laws, and fundamentalist religious groups allied with neoconservative reaction in the mainline churches keep the legislative process at a standstill, well behind developments in European states. It is this passivity that contributes to the violence of injustice and establishes the environment to which the San Francisco Task Force was speaking.

Camara's analysis of the three forms of violence was addressed to conditions of the world's poor in less-developed third world countries rather than to the subject of sexuality. Although it is especially pertinent to the third and final criterion of the future of a liberated sexuality, I must say in the present context that the establishment of a nonviolent sexual life-style is rendered enormously more difficult in an environment of heightening political violence.

Sexual love that fulfills and enriches human relationships is based on mutuality, the gentle and caressing touch, responsiveness to and tenderness toward the other—what can be called "software." But the affairs of nations are carried out with hardware of the most lethal sort, the hallowing of martial virtues and heralding of the heroic violence prevailing over the malicious violence of each successive enemy. We too have buggered the Persians, and the people are tutored in the glory of it. By the balance of terror ideology and the nuclear hardware created to make it "work," the world has evolved into a constant readiness and willingness to destroy in only a few moments of time hundreds of millions of people even less responsible than we in the so-called democratic societies for the unchallenged tyranny of hardware civilization and the corresponding denial of the culture of nonviolent love.

So much does this state of readiness for instant orgasms of vio-

[46]The history of this legislation is narrated by Peter Coleman, *Christian Attitudes to Homosexuality* (London: SPCK, 1980), pp. 159–82. See also John Wolfenden, chairperson, *The Wolfenden Report,* introduction by Karl Menninger (New York: Stein & Day, 1963), pp. 42–48.

lence now prevail that we are unexpectedly returned to the moral mood of first-century apocalypse. When Williams, therefore, seeks to provide a guarded sanction, on the basis of *agapē*, for the possession and use of nuclear weapons, it is a reasoning that seems to contradict in the political domain what he wants to establish in the ethic of sexual love liberated by *agapē*.[47] Thus the transformative power of love comes to us in a revelatory (i.e., apocalyptic) manner to break the circle of violence described by Camara. For this reason the failure of politics to end the circle of violence now dragging the nations downward into poverty, bloodshed, and death must be overcome if a nonviolent sexuality is to bless the human future.

3. *Transgenital awareness* attempts to place sexuality in appropriate relationship to the total moral task of liberating love. Men and women do not live by sex alone. To designate someone "a homosexual" usually means to give that person a genital identity to which everything else is subordinate. Gay/lesbian liberation is the overcoming of this genital stereotype, establishing personhood beyond the confines of sexual functions. At stake in transgenital awareness is the placing of sexuality in a total spectrum of moral challenges pertinent to human liberation and impinging on sexuality in such a way that its growth toward completeness, its history, is without them stunted.

The character of transgenital awareness is taken once again from the paradigm of *agapē* in the context of 1 Corinthians 12—14. Pneumaticism produced at Corinth a triumphal fixation on ecstatic phenomena that led not to freedom but to chaotic fragmentation. In face of this deteriorative situation 1 Corinthians 12—14 ethicizes the Spirit and brings its manifestations down from the clouds of personalized euphoria into the painful struggle for community wholeness in the "body" of Christ. Paul's style of sociologicial criticism is particularly distinctive in this context. It instructs the Corinthian enthusiasts in another agenda to which they are responsible not merely in a pragmatic, administrative sense based on "the more we get together, the happier we'll be" but in the Christological sense that the church constituted as church by the bodily suffering of Christ is called thereby to hear the world's groaning for liberation

---

[47] Williams, *The Spirit and the Forms of Love*, pp. 270–72.

from bondage (Romans 8:18–21) and enter into it with collaborative effort. The church, even at worship (1 Corinthians 12—14), is thus called out of an erotic, self-centered piety into concert with the groaning heard within the whole of creation.[48]

J. Christian Beker has observed that Christ crucified (1 Corinthians 2:2) "is not brought into the argument in 1 Corinthians 12—14," and this is anomolous because Paul elsewhere (cf. 2 Corinthians 5:14–15; Galatians 2:19–20) "derives Christian love from the death of Christ as the act of God's love."[49] Beker goes on to affirm that "the cruciform nature of the Spirit remains inchoate in Paul, . . . because the Spirit refers primarily to the victory of the risen Christ over sin and death, which as the power of the future moves us to the apocalyptic glory of God."[50] Although it is correct that the Christological foundation of *agapē* is not explicit in 1 Corinthians 13, it is unmistakable in 1 Corinthians 1—4 and must be brought to the aid of historical exegesis at chapter 13. To say this in terms of content criticism, what Paul *means* must be used to clarify what he says if the moral power of Christian belief is to be translated into contemporary life experience. This is also true with respect to Beker's comment on the Spirit, the victory of Christ, and the coming apocalypse. That is, we must ask about the moral content of this triumph and how this apocalypse translates into social ministry in a time of liberation theology.

There is, furthermore, a second, secular sense in which the very absence of the cross-centered kerygma in 1 Corinthians 13 may be instructive for the Christian understanding of social ethics in general as over against biblical ethics or Christian ethics in particular. That is, the moral task from the confessional standpoint is clearly an imperative that derives from an indicative. The first "word" of the decalogue (Exodus 20:2) is the Exodus confession (the Lord brought you out), the indicative of deliverance from which the other "words" proceed. Paul's "word of the cross" (1 Corinthians 1:18) is similarly the indicative from which the moral instructions of the Corinthian correspondence proceed.

---

[48] What Käsemann says about Romans 8 in "The Cry for Liberty in the Worship of the Church," *Perspectives on Paul*, pp. 122–37, correctly includes the parallel situation in 1 Corinthians 12—14.

[49] J. Christian Beker, *Paul the Apostle* (Philadelphia: Fortress Press, 1980), pp. 291–92.

[50] Ibid., p. 294.

Biblical faith is not embarrassed by or discontent with the complementarity of these two features and would not be hopeful about a moral vision cut off from confessional premises. The absence of the normative Pauline kerygma in 1 Corinthians 13, however, makes possible a sympathetic hearing of the cosmic travail toward liberation in its multifarious manifestations (Romans 8:22) and provides a mode through which confessional faith can relate responsibly to these manifestations and facilitate their fruition. It is also true—especially so in the case of the gay/lesbian attitude toward the church—that the false piety of the church is so alienating that secular forms of love may, in some settings, become the necessary manifestation of the love of God. In short, this means that love, without becoming antisexual, is carried beyond the perimeters of sexuality itself into the total arena of the liberation struggle.

It should be reaffirmed in the elaboration of this theme that homosexual orientation is no more genitally focused than heterosexual orientation. Whatever accuracy may be ascribed to statistical measurements of sexual activity, Stephen Morin and Ellen Garfinkle report among homosexual men 1.3 orgasms per week, with three per week among heterosexual men.[51]

In a society in which *Playboy* foldouts become standard forms of popular art and the female as sex object becomes a pervasive ingredient in cinema and commerce, it is understandable that gay/lesbian sexuality should be viewed with exaggerated ideas of genital virility. What is different is xenophobically perceived as threat. The fact is that "sexist" has its original meaning in a dynamic field of male/female relationships in which the female is reduced to a set of genital functions and expectations in a hierarchy of male power. The task of liberating love is to transcend this reductionism, to enter into the total range of effort through which the human prospect is unfolding, to underline the confluence in the love of God of the totality of human passions for freedom.

At the 1977 Houston assembly of the National Women's Conference, Betty Friedan met the appeal of lesbian women in a way well illustrating the point I want to make:

---

[51] Stephen Morin and Ellen G. Garfinkle, "Male Homophobia," in James Chesebro, ed., *Gayspeak* (New York: Pilgrim Press, 1981), p. 121. The statistics come apparently from Alfred Kinsey, W.B. Pomeroy, and C.E. Martin, *Sexual Behavior in the Human Male* (Philadelphia: W.B. Saunders, 1948), p. 261, table 58, figs. 83–88; pp. 268–69, table 60, figs. 50–52.

I had strongly objected to the confusion of feminism with lesbianism and to focusing on lesbian rights to the neglect of issues of equality common to all women. But now I objected even more strongly to the way the right wing was trying to fan a hysteria of hate and fear against homosexuals, to cloak their real economic and political objections to the Equal Rights Amendment. It would have been immoral, wrong, to sacrifice the civil rights of the lesbians to appease the right wing.[52]

Transgenital awareness is an essential element of the politics of liberation. At the same time it requires a transvaluation of politics itself. It is not difficult to deduce the reasons for exclusion of lesbian claims from the struggle for women's rights. To include them would divide the voting constituency and thus diminish the legislative strength necessary for the passing of the Equal Rights Amendment. Indeed, it could be said, in face of the negative outcome of the ERA struggle in the early 1980s, that the agenda of the women lacked focus and aided its own defeat by failing to exclude lesbian demands for which the public and the politicians, in particular, are not prepared.

It is certainly true that one-issue politics is capable of greater emotional intensity and organizational coherence. Within a narrowed conception of the public good it can also produce larger records of electoral success. People like to think they are "getting somewhere." But we are faced today with a significant anomaly: a list of piecemeal political achievements and a simultaneous cynicism about the political process itself as an instrument of the public good.

There is ground for believing that the character of politics, resting solidly as it does on the pragmatic criterion of what is feasible or what "works," becomes, in the process, such a constriction of reality from the moral standpoint that its effectiveness as an instrument of human liberation is correspondingly abridged. It is obvious that liberation theology in the Latin American sense came into prominence in the presence of an all-male priesthood and was predominantly responsive to the oppressive hegemony of indigenous economic oligarchies reinforced by the military-industrial complex of the United States. It is difficult for this specific constellation of formative forces to stand in meaningful relationship with the women's movement or the black movement, to cite only two con-

[52] Betty Friedan, "The Women at Houston," *The New Republic* 177 (December 10, 1977):18.

stituencies of the struggle for liberation in North America.[53] The consequence of the political process, therefore, is usually that of division among those seeking significant social change through normal political channels. Fred Herzog has appropriately warned that this division is an intentional tactic of forces opposed to liberation.[54] By such division, reformist tendencies can be absorbed within the dominant political structures and accommodated in such ways that structural injustice is only modestly affected. Golda Meir, Indira Gandhi, and Margaret Thatcher effectively illustrate how women can achieve significant electoral successes and serve quite well the politics of the status quo. In the political process, liberation usually becomes "development" and produces disbelief among those it is designed to benefit.

On April 4, 1967, at Riverside Church in New York City, Martin Luther King Jr. condemned the war in Vietnam to the consternation of those who had hoped to contain the civil rights movement of the 1960s within the realm of domestic American politics. One could view this as an unwise deviation from the civil rights of black people, since indeed a significant (even disproportionate) number of blacks was fighting and dying in Vietnam and since many black people have found within the military employment and career opportunities not otherwise accessible. It is certain that King's excur-

[53]There is an interesting story about "Women's Liberation Latin American Style" in Esther Arias and Mortimer Arias, *The Cry of My People: Out of Captivity in Latin America* (New York: Friendship Press, 1980), pp. 82–100. This story has to do with the experience of a Bolivian woman, Domitila Barrios de Chungara, wife of a Bolivian miner and General Secretary of the Asociacion de Amas de Casa (Housekeepers Association) at the International Women's Year Conference sponsored by the United Nations in Mexico City in 1975. Coming from an anguishing struggle of impoverished Bolivian workers in constant conflict with the ruling Bolivian junta, Domitila is deeply angered by the upper-class style (mode of dress, transportation, etc.) of the North American feminist leadership and the inclusion of prostitutes and lesbians in the agenda of the nongovernmental organizations whose deliberations she had been invited to share. Finally, Domitila leads a group of Latin American women to separate from the planned program in order to deal with the *real* agenda: "Getting our country [Bolivia] liberated from the imperialist yoke." She refuses to hear Betty Friedan's appeal for solidarity with the main conference. Since prostitutes and lesbians are put together (along with standard North American feminist interests) as repugnant irrelevancies, it is not surprising that the discussion of "Women's Liberation Latin American Style" becomes an oblique apology for the kind of feminism we read about in Marabel Morgan's *Total Woman* (Old Tappan, NJ: Fleming H. Revell, 1973)! Domitila tells her side of the story in Domitila Barrios de Chungara, *Let Me Speak!* (New York: Monthly Review, 1978).
[54]Fred Herzog, *Justice Church: The New Function of the Church in North American Christianity* (Maryknoll, NY: Orbis Books, 1980), pp. 15–18.

sion into international affairs turned away elements of support positive on black liberation but negative on the self-determination of the Vietnamese. One year after King's break with American Vietnam policy he was murdered by an assassin in Memphis, Tennessee. Some are prone to say that leadership had already passed from his hands to others who could more "authentically" represent the needs of black people in the United States.

Another way to view King's "unpolitical" adoption of the peace agenda in 1967 is that it was the inevitable result of the unfolding in his own conscience of the power of *agapē*. It was the realization that *agapē* does not compartmentalize human concerns so that the pursuit of one or a portion of such concerns grants us exemption from the rest of them. The human condition in our time is such that fragments of freedom, bits and pieces of wholeness, and islands of well-being must open themselves to the total human outcry against violence and oppression and must resist every segmentation that makes our specific social concern oblivious or unrelated to others whose consciousness of freedom is not similarly shaped. This is inherent in what is meant by transgenital awareness as a criterion of liberating love.

The parable of the good Samaritan (Luke 10:29–37) appears as an appendix to a synoptic tradition (Mark 12:28–31/Matthew 22:34–40/ Luke 10:25–28) that elevates the love of God and the love of neighbor to the supreme rank of moral concern. Because the parable is unique to Luke and bears so many specifically Lucan characteristics, it has seemed doubtful to me for many years that the parable is an original saying of Jesus, despite its religious and moral profundity. It is, however, an illustration of the task inherent in *agapē* as the power of liberating love at work in human affairs.

The story begins with the question, Who is my neighbor? This question rests on an ethic of parochialism that enables one to set the limits of responsibility: to include certain people, to leave others out. It encourages me to believe that Christian tradition in the spirit of Jesus, in the spirit of *agapē*, took the question of segmented concern in hand and answered it in Christ's name. The parable follows out the implications of *agapē* in the new situation contemporaneous with Luke the evangelist. Letha Scanzoni and Virginia Mollenkott followed the lead of this parable in their discussion of the question, *Is the Homosexual My Neighbor?*[55] The answer is

[55] (San Francisco: Harper & Row, 1978).

obviously yes. The future of gay/lesbian liberation lies not only in its ability unitedly to pursue justice for homosexual people but also in its ability to embrace in love the outcry for freedom among all people, whether near or far. It is, furthermore, responsiveness to this same outcry that gives to sexuality in general its appropriate place in the total human prospect.

BIBLIOGRAPHY

Altman, Dennis. *Homosexual Oppression and Liberation.* New York: Avon Books, 1971.

Anderson, Bernard W. *Understanding the Old Testament.* 3d ed. Englewood Cliffs, NJ: Prentice-Hall, 1975.

Arias, Esther, and Mortimer Arias. *The Cry of My People: Out of Captivity in Latin America.* New York: Friendship Press, 1980.

Aristotle. *Poetics.* Ed. and trans. S.H. Butler. 3d ed. London: Macmillan, 1902.

Athanasius. *Contra Gentes and De Incarnatione.* Ed. and trans. Robert W. Thompson. Oxford: Clarendon Press, 1971.

Bailey, D.S. *Homosexuality and the Western Christian Tradition.* London: Longmans, Green, 1955.

Barrett, C.K. *A Commentary on the Epistle to the Romans.* Harper's New Testament Commentaries. New York: Harper & Bros., 1957.

———. *The Gospel According to St. John.* 2d ed. Philadelphia: Westminster Press, 1978.

Barton, George A. "Sodomy." In *Encyclopaedia of Religion and Ethics.* Ed. James Hastings. New York: Charles Scribner's Sons, 1921. 11:672–74.

Batchelor, Edward Jr., ed. *Homosexuality and Ethics.* New York: The Pilgrim Press, 1980.

Bauer, Walter, F.W. Gingrich, and F.W. Danker. *A Greek-English Lexicon of the New Testament.* 2d ed. Chicago: University of Chicago Press, 1979.

Baur, F.C. "Über Zweck und Veranlassung des Römerbriefs und die damit zusammenhängenden Verhältnisse der römischen Gemeinde." *Ausgewählte Werke in Einzelausgaben.* Bd. 1. Hrsg. v. Klaus Scholder. Einf. v. E. Käsemann. Stuttgart: Friedrich Frommann, 1963. Pp. 147–266.

Beker, J. Christian. *Paul the Apostle.* Philadelphia: Fortress Press, 1980.

Bell, Alan P., and Martin S. Weinberg. *Homosexualities: A Study of Diversity Among Men and Women.* New York: Simon & Schuster, 1978.

Bell, Alan P., Martin S. Weinberg, and Sue K. Hammersmith. *Sexual Preference: Its Development in Men and Women.* 2 vols. Bloomington: Indiana University Press, 1981.

Berger, Klaus, *Exegese des Neuen Testaments*. Uni-Taschenbuch 658. Heidelberg: Quelle & Meyer, 1977.

Bergman, Jan, A.O. Haldar, and Gerhard Wallis. ᵓ*ahabh*, ktl. *Theological Dictionary of the Old Testament*. Ed. G. Johannes Botterweck and Helmer Ringgren; trans. J.T. Willis. Grand Rapids, MI: Wm. B. Eerdmans., 1974. 1:99–118.

Betz, Hans D. *Galatians*. Hermeneia. Philadelphia: Fortress Press, 1979.

Bloch, Ernst. *Das Prinzip Hoffnung*. Gesamtausgabe. Bd. 5. Frankfurt am Main: Suhrkamp, 1959.

Boling, Robert G. *Judges*. The Anchor Bible. New York: Doubleday, 1975.

Bornkamm, Günther. *Early Christian Experience*. Trans. Paul L. Hammer. New York: Harper & Row, 1969.

――――. "Formen und Gattungen." *Die Religion in Geschichte und Gegenwart*. Hrsg. Kurt Galling. 3. Aufl. Tübingen: J.C.B. Mohr, 1958. 3:999–1005.

Boswell, John. *Christianity, Social Tolerance, and Homosexuality*. Chicago: University of Chicago Press, 1980.

Bowra, C.M. "Sappho." In *Oxford Classical Dictionary*. 2d ed. Ed. N.G.L. Hammond and H.H. Sculland. Oxford: Clarendon Press, 1970. pp. 950–51.

Bright, John. *Jeremiah*. The Anchor Bible. New York: Doubleday, 1965.

Brooks, Beatrice A. "Fertility Cult Functionaries in the Old Testament." *Journal of Biblical Literature* 60 (1941):227–53.

Brown, Francis, S.R. Driver, and C.A. Briggs, eds. *A Hebrew and English Lexicon of the Old Testament*. New York: Houghton Mifflin, 1955.

Brown, Robert McAfee. *Making Peace in the Global Village*. Philadelphia: Westminster Press, 1978.

――――. *Theology in a New Key*. Philadelphia: Westminster Press, 1981.

Budde, Karl. *Das Buch der Richter*. Kurzer Hand-Kommentar zum Alten Testament. Tübingen: J.C.B. Mohr, 1897.

Bultmann, Rudolf. "Glossen im Römerbrief." *Theologische Literaturzeitung* 72 (1947):197–202.

――――. "Is Exegesis Without Presuppositions Possible?" *Existence and Faith*. Trans. Schubert Ogden. New York: Meridian, 1960. Pp. 289–96.

――――. *The Johannine Epistles*. Trans. R.P. O'Hara and others. Hermeneia. Philadelphia: Fortress Press, 1973.

――――. "Das Problem einer theologischen Exegese des Neuen Testaments," *Zwischen den Zeiten* 3 (1925):337–57.

――――. *Theology of the New Testament*. Vol. 1. Trans. K. Grobel. New York: Macmillan, 1952.

Burchfield, R.W., ed. *A Supplement to the Oxford English Dictionary*. Vol. 2, H–N. Oxford: Clarendon Press, 1976.

Burney, C.F. *The Book of Judges*. 2d ed. London: Rivingtons, 1930.

Charles, R.H. *The Apocrypha and Pseudepigrapha of the Old Testament.* Vol. 2 of Pseudepigrapha. Oxford: Clarendon Press, 1913.

Chesebro, James, ed. *Gayspeak: Gay Male and Lesbian Communication.* New York: The Pilgrim Press, 1981.

Chrysostom, St. John. "Homilies on the Acts of the Apostles and the Epistle to the Romans." *Nicene and Post-Nicene Fathers.* Ed. Philip Schaff. Grand Rapids, MI: Wm. B. Eerdmans, 1956. 11:355–59.

de Chungara, Domitila Barrios. *Let Me Speak!* New York: Monthly Review, 1978.

Clemons, James T. "Toward a Christian Affirmation of Human Sexuality." *Religion in Life* 43 (1974):425–35.

Coleman, Peter. *Christian Attitudes to Homosexuality.* London: SPCK, 1980.

Cone, James. *A Black Theology of Liberation.* Philadelphia: J.B. Lippincott, 1970.

Conzelmann, Hans. *1 Corinthians.* Trans. James W. Leitch and ed. George M. MacRae. Hermeneia. Philadelphia: Fortress Press, 1975.

———. "Korinth und die Mädchen der Aphrodite," *Nachrichten der Wissenschaften in Göttingen* 8 (1967–68):247–61.

Conzelmann, Hans, und A. Lindemann. *Arbeitsbuch zum Neuen Testament.* 3. Aufl. Uni-Taschenbuch 52. Tübingen: J.C.B. Mohr, 1977.

Coote, Robert B. *Amos Among the Prophets.* Philadelphia: Fortress Press, 1981.

Creighton, C. "Leprosy, Leper." In *Encyclopaedia Biblica.* Ed. T.K. Cheyne and J.S. Black. New York: Macmillan, 1902. III: 2763–68.

Daly, Mary. *Beyond God the Father.* Boston: Beacon Press, 1973.

Deissmann, Adolf. *Light from the Ancient East.* Trans. L.R.M. Strachan. Rev. ed. London: Hodder and Stoughton, 1927.

Dibelius, Martin, and Hans Conzelmann. *The Pastoral Epistles.* Trans. P. Buttolph and A. Yarbro. Hermeneia. Philadelphia: Fortress Press, 1972.

Dio Chrysostom. *Discourses.* Vol. 5. Trans. H. Lamar Crosby. Loeb Classical Library. Cambridge, MA: Harvard University Press, 1951.

Dobbie, Robert. "Deuteronomy and the Prophetic Attitude to Sacrifice." *Scottish Journal of Theology* 12 (1959):68–82.

Dodd, C.H. *The Epistle of Paul to the Romans.* Moffatt New Testament Commentary, 1932. Reprint. London: Hodder and Stoughton, 1947.

Douglas, Mary. "Critique and Commentary." In Jacob Neusner, *The Idea of Purity in Ancient Judaism.* Leiden: E.J. Brill, 1973. Pp. 137–42.

Dover, Kenneth J. "Classical Attitudes to Sexual Behaviour." *Arethusa* 6 (1973):59–73.

———. *Greek Homosexuality.* Cambridge, MA: Harvard University Press, 1978.

———. Letter to George R. Edwards. October 26, 1982.

————. ed. Plato's *Symposium*. London: Cambridge University Press, 1980.

Driver, S.R. *A Critical and Exegetical Commentary on Deuteronomy*. 3d ed. International Critical Commentary. Edinburgh: T & T Clark, 1902.

Easton, B.S. "New Testament Ethical Lists." *Journal of Biblical Literature* 51 (1932):1–12.

Eichrodt, Walter. *Ezekiel: A Commentary*. Trans. Crosslett Quinn. Old Testament Library. Philadelphia: Westminster Press, 1970.

Eissfeldt, Otto. *The Old Testament: An Introduction*. Trans. Peter R. Ackroyd. New York: Harper & Row, 1965.

Enslin, Morton S. *The Ethic of Paul*. New York: Harper & Bros., 1930.

Farrar, Frederic W. *History of Interpretation*. London: Macmillan, 1886.

Fields, Cheryl M. "Six Universities Could Lose Defense Contracts over Law School Bans on Army Recruiters." *The Chronicle of Higher Education* 24 (August 4, 1982):1.

Fohrer, Georg. *History of Israelite Religion*. Trans. David Green. Nashville: Abingdon Press, 1973.

————. *Introduction to the Old Testament*. Trans. David Green. Nashville: Abingdon Press, 1968.

Freedman, David N. "Deuteronomic History, The." In *Interpreter's Dictionary of the Bible Supplement*. Ed. Keith Crim and others. Nashville: Abingdon Press, 1976. Pp. 226–28.

Freud, Sigmund. *Three Essays on the Theory of Sexuality*. Trans. and ed. James Strachey. London: Hogarth, 1974.

Friedan, Betty. "The Women at Houston." *The New Republic* 177 (December 10, 1977):15–19.

Fromm, Erich. *The Anatomy of Human Destructiveness*. New York: Holt, Rinehart & Winston, 1973.

————. *May Man Prevail?* New York: Doubleday, 1961.

Fuller, R.H. *A Critical Introduction to the New Testament*. London: Duckworth, 1966.

Furnish, Victor Paul. *The Moral Teaching of Paul*. Nashville: Abingdon Press, 1979.

————. *Theology and Ethics in Paul*. Nashville: Abingdon Press, 1968.

Georges, Karl E., und Heinrich Georges, Hrsg. *Lateinisch-Deutsches Handwörterbuch*. 11. Aufl. 2. Bd. Basel: Benno Schwabe, 1962.

Gesenius, Wilhelm. *Handwörterbuch über das Alte Testament*. 14. Aufl. Hrsg. v. H. Zimmern u. F. Buhl. Leipzig: F.C.W. Vogel, 1905.

————. *Hebrew and English Lexicon of the Old Testament*. Ed. F. Brown, S.R. Driver, C.A. Briggs. Oxford: Clarendon Press, 1907.

Gibbon, Edward. *The Decline and Fall of the Roman Empire*. Ed. O. Smeaton. Vol. 4. New York: E.P. Dutton, 1910.

Gibson, E. Lawrence. *Get Off My Ship: Ensign Berg vs. the U.S. Navy*. New York: Avon Books, 1978.

Gonzales, Justo L., and Catherine C. Gonzales. *Liberation Preaching*. Nashville: Abingdon Press, 1980.

Gordon, Kevin, chpsn. *Homosexuality and Social Justice*. San Francisco: Task Force on Gay/Lesbian Issues, Commission on Social Justice, Archdiocese of San Francisco, July 1982.

Gottwald, Norman. *A Light to the Nations*. New York: Harper & Bros., 1959.

———. *The Tribes of Yahweh: A Sociology of the Religion of Liberated Israel, 1250–1050 B.C.* Maryknoll, NY: Orbis Books, 1979.

Gray, John. *I and II Kings*. 2d ed. Old Testament Library. Philadelphia: Westminster Press, 1970.

Grenfell, Bernard P., and Arthur S. Hunt, eds. *The Hibeh Papyrus*. Part 1. London: Kegan Paul, French, Trübner, 1906.

Grim, Jacob, und Wilhelm Grimm, Hrsg. *Deutsches Wörterbuch*. Bd. 5. Leipzig: S. Hirzel, 1873.

Gunkel, Hermann. *Genesis*. 3. Aufl. Göttinger Handkommentar zum Alten Testament. Göttingen: Vandenhoeck & Ruprecht, 1910.

Gutiérrez, Gustavo. *A Theology of Liberation*. Trans. and ed. Sister Caridad Inda and John Eagelson. Peru, 1971; Maryknoll, NY: Orbis Books, 1973.

Hanson, A.T. *The Wrath of the Lamb*. London: SPCK, 1957.

Harlan, J.P. "Sodom." In *Interpreter's Dictionary of the Bible*. Ed. G.A. Buttrick and others. Nashville: Abingdon Press, 1962. Vol. R–Z: 395–97.

Harrison, Beverly W. "Misogyny and Homophobia: The Unexplored Connections." *Church and Society* 72 (November/December 1982):20–33.

Hauck, Friedrich, and Siegfried Schulz. *Pornē, pornos, ktl. Theological Dictionary of the New Testament*. Ed. G. Friedrich; trans. and ed. G.W. Bromiley. Grand Rapids, MI: Wm. B. Eerdmans, 1968. 6:579–97.

Heger, Heinz. *The Men with the Pink Triangle*. Trans. David Fernbach. Boston: Alyson Publications, 1980.

Heiler, Friedrich. *Die Frau in den Religionen der Menschheit*. New York: Walter de Gruyter, 1977.

Herodotus, *History*. Trans. A.D. Godley. Loeb Classical Library. Cambridge, MA: Harvard University Press, 1946. I:250–53.

Heron, Alastair. "Towards a Christian View of Sex." In *Homosexuality and Ethics*. Ed. E. Batchelor, Jr. New York: Pilgrim Press, 1980. Pp. 135–38.

Herzog, Fred. *Justice Church: The New Function of the Church in North American Christianity*. Maryknoll, NY: Orbis Books, 1980.

Humbert, Paul. "Le substantiv to‘ēbā et le verbe t‘b dans l'Ancien Testament." *Zeitschrift für die alttestamentliche Wissenschaft* 72 (1960): 217–37.

James, M.R. *The Apocryphal New Testament*. Oxford: Clarendon Press, 1953.

————. *The Second Epistle of Peter and the General Epistle of Jude.* Cambridge Greek Testament. Cambridge: Cambridge University Press, 1912.

Jewett, Robert. "Romans as an Ambassadorial Letter." *Interpretation* 36 (1982):5–20.

Josephus, Flavius. *Jewish Antiquities.* Vol. 4. Trans. H. St. J. Thackeray. Loeb Classical Library. Cambridge, MA: Harvard University Press, 1967.

————. *The Works of Flavius Josephus.* Vol. 1. Trans. William Whiston. Philadelphia: J. Grigg, 1831.

Kamlah, Ehrhard. *Die Form der katalogischen Paränese im Neuen Testament.* Wissenschaftliche Untersuchungen zum Neuen Testament 7. Tübingen: J.C.B. Mohr, 1964.

Käsemann, Ernst. *Commentary on Romans.* Trans. and ed. G.W. Bromiley. Grand Rapids, MI: Wm. B. Eerdmans, 1980.

————. *Jesus Means Freedom.* Trans. Frank Clarke. Philadelphia: Fortress Press, 1969.

————. *Leib und Leib Christi: Eine Untersuchung zur paulinischen Begrifflichkeit.* Beiträge zur historischen Theologie. Tübingen: J.C.B. Mohr, 1933.

————. *Perspectives on Paul.* Trans. Margaret Kohl. Philadelphia: Fortress Press, 1971.

Katchadourian, Herant A., and Donald T. Lunde. *Fundamentals of Human Sexuality.* 2d ed. New York: Holt, Rinehart & Winston, 1975.

Keck, L.E. and G.M. Tucker. "Exegesis." In *Interpreter's Dictionary of the Bible Supplement.* Ed. Keith Crim and others. Nashville: Abingdon Press, 1976. Pp. 296–303.

Keil, Carl F. *Biblischer Commentar über die Bücher Mose's.* 2. Bd. *Leviticus, Numbri und Deuteronomium.* Leipzig: Dörffling und Franke, 1862.

Kinsey, Alfred, W.B. Pomeroy, and C.E. Martin. *Sexual Behavior in the Human Male.* Philadelphia: W.B. Saunders, 1948.

————, W.B. Pomeroy, C.E. Martin, and P.H. Gebhard. *Sexual Behavior in the Human Female.* Philadelphia: W.B. Saunders, 1953.

Klostermann, E. *Kleine Texte fuer theologische Vorlesungen und Uebungen.* Nr. 3. Bonn: A. Marcus und E. Weber, 1908.

Krafft-Ebing, Richard. *Psychopathia Sexualis.* Trans. C.G. Chaddock. Philadelphia: F.A. Davis, 1892.

Kroll, Wilhelm. "Knabenliebe." In *Paulys Realencyclopaedia der classischen Altertumswissenschaft.* Hrsg. v. Georg Wissowa und Wilhelm Kroll. Stuttgart: J.B. Metzler, 1921. 21:897–906.

Kümmel, Werner G. *Introduction to the New Testament.* Rev. ed. Trans. Howard C. Kee. Nashville: Abingdon Press, 1975.

Lang, Daniel. *The Casualties of War.* New York: McGraw-Hill, 1969.

Lara-Braud, Jorge. *What Is Liberation Theology?* Atlanta: General Assembly Mission Board, Presbyterian Church in the United States, 1980.

Lewis, Bill. "The Real Gay Epidemic: Panic and Paranoia." *Body Politic* 88 (November 1982):38–40.

Lewis, Charlton T., and Charles Short. *A Latin Dictionary.* Oxford: Clarendon Press, 1966.

Lieberson, Jonathan. "Anatomy of an Epidemic." *New York Review of Books* 30 (August 18, 1983):17–22.

Lietzmann, Hans. *An die Römer.* 5. Aufl. Handbuch zum Neuen Testament. Hrsg. v. G. Bornkamm. Tübingen: J.C.B. Mohr, 1971.

Lucian. *Lucius or the Ass.* Trans. M.D. Macleod. Loeb Classical Library. Cambridge, MA: Harvard University Press, 1967. 5:110–14.

Lyles, J.C. "The Unity They Seek." *Christian Century* 100 (1983):539–40.

Lynch, Michael. "Living with Kaposi's." *Body Politic* 88 (November 1982): 31–37.

Macgregor, G.H.C. "The Concept of the Wrath of God in the New Testament." *New Testament Studies* 7 (1960/61):101–9.

McNeill, John J. *The Church and the Homosexual.* Kansas City: Sheed Andrews and McMeel, 1976.

Mannheim, Karl. *Ideology and Utopia.* Trans. L. Wirth and E. Shils. New York: Harcourt, Brace, and World, 1936.

Manson, William. *The Epistle to the Hebrews.* London: Hodder and Stoughton, 1951.

Marotta, Toby. *The Politics of Homosexuality.* Boston: Houghton Mifflin, 1981.

Marrou, Henrì-Irénée. *Histoire de l'education dans l'antiquite.* 6th ed. Paris: Editions de Seuil, 1965.

Masters, William, and Virginia Johnson. *Homosexuality in Perspective.* Boston: Little, Brown, 1979.

Mauser, Ulrich. *Gottesbild und Menschwerdung.* Beiträge zur historischen Theologie 43. Tübingen: J.C.B. Mohr, 1971.

Mellaart, J. *Çatal Hüyük: A Neolithic Town in Anatolia.* New York: McGraw-Hill, 1967.

Michel, Otto. *Der Brief an die Römer.* 4. Aufl. Meyers kritisch-exegetischer Kommentar über Das Neuen Testament. Göttingen: Vandenhoeck & Ruprecht, 1966.

Miranda, José. *Being and the Messiah: The Message of St. John.* Trans. John Eagelson. Maryknoll, NY: Orbis Books, 1977.

———. *Marx Against the Marxists: The Christian Humanism of Karl Marx.* Trans. John Drury. Maryknoll, NY: Orbis Books, 1980.

———. *Marx and the Bible: A Critique of the Philosophy of Oppression.* Trans. John Eagelson. Maryknoll, NY: Orbis Books, 1974.

Mish, F.C., and others, eds. *Webster's Ninth New Collegiate Dictionary.* Springfield, MA: Merriam-Webster, 1983.

Moltmann-Wendel, Elisabeth. *Liberty, Equality, Sisterhood.* Trans. Ruth Gritsch. Philadelphia: Fortress Press, 1978.

Moore, George F. *Judges.* International Critical Commentary. 7th ed. Edinburgh: T & T Clark, 1895.

Morgan, Marabel. *Total Woman.* Old Tappen, NJ: Fleming H. Revell, 1973.

Morin, Stephen, and Ellen G. Garfinkle. "Male Homophobia." In *Gayspeak.* Ed. James W. Chesebro, pp. 117–29. New York: Pilgrim Press, 1981.

Murray, John. *The Epistle to the Romans.* New International Commentary on the New Testament. Grand Rapids, MI: Wm. B. Eerdmans, 1959.

Nelson, James B. *Embodiment. An Approach to Sexuality and Christian Theology.* Minneapolis: Augsburg, 1978.

————. "Gayness and Homosexuality: Issues for the Church." In *Homosexuality and Ethics.* Ed. E. Batchelor, Jr. New York: Pilgrim Press, 1980. Pp. 186–210.

Neusner, Jacob. *The Idea of Purity in Ancient Judaism.* Leiden: E.J. Brill, 1973.

Noth, Martin. *Leviticus: A Commentary.* Rev. ed. Ed. and trans. J.E. Anderson. Old Testament Library. Philadelphia: Westminster Press, 1977.

————. *Überlieferungsgeschichtliche Studien.* Vol. 1. Halle: Niemeyer, 1943.

Nowack, W. *Richter, Ruth und Bücher Samuelis.* Handkommentar zum Alten Testament. Göttingen: Vandenhoeck & Ruprecht, 1902.

Nygren, Anders. *Agape and Eros.* Rev. ed. Trans. P.S. Watson. Philadelphia: Westminster Press, 1953.

————. *Commentary on Romans.* Trans. Carl C. Rasmussen. Philadelphia: Muhlenberg Press, 1949.

Pfeiffer, Robert. *Introduction to the Old Testament.* New York: Harper & Bros., 1941.

Philo. *On Abraham.* Vol. 6. Trans. F.H. Colson. Loeb Classical Library. Cambridge, MA: Harvard University Press, 1935.

Pittenger, Norman. "The Morality of Homosexual Acts." In *Homosexuality and Ethics.* Ed. E. Batchelor Jr. New York: The Pilgrim Press, 1980. Pp. 139–53.

Plato. *Symposium.* Ed. Kenneth J. Dover. London: Cambridge University Press, 1980.

Plato. *Symposium.* Vol. 5 of Plato *(Lysis, Symposium, Gorgias).* Trans. W.R.M. Lamb. Loeb Classical Library. Cambridge, MA: Harvard Univ., 1925.

Plutarch. *Moralia.* Vol. 9 *(Dialogue on Love).* Trans. W.C. Helmbold. Loeb Classical Library. Cambridge, MA: Harvard University Press, 1961.

Plautus. *The Braggart Warrior.* Vol. 3 of Plautus. Trans. Paul Nixon, Loeb Classical Library. New York: G.P. Putnam's Sons, 1924.

Pope, Marvin. *Job.* 3d ed. The Anchor Bible. New York: Doubleday, 1973.

Quell, Gottfried, and Ethelbert Stauffer. Agapaō, ktl. *Theological Diction-ary of the New Testament*. Ed. Gerhard Kittel; trans. and ed. G.W. Bromiley. Grand Rapids, MI: Wm. B. Eerdmans, 1968. 1:21–55.

von Rad, Gerhard. *Genesis: A Commentary*. Rev. ed. Trans. John H. Marks. Old Testament Library. Philadelphia: Westminster Press, 1972.

Ramsay, William M. *The Cities and Bishoprics of Phrygia*. Vol. 1. Oxford: Clarendon Press, 1895.

Rechy, John. "An Exchange on AIDS." *New York Review of Books* 30 (October 13, 1983):43–45.

Reicke, Bo. *The General Epistles of James, Peter, and Jude*. The Anchor Bible. New York: Doubleday, 1964.

Rühle, Oskar. "Prostitution: I. Heilige Prostitution." *Die Religion in Ge-schichte und Gegenwart*. 2. Aufl. Hrsg. H. Gunkel und L. Zscharnack. Tübingen: J.C.B. Mohr, 1930. IV: 1576–77.

Sanday, William, and H.C. Headlam. *A Critical and Exegetical Commen-tary on the Epistle to the Romans*. 5th ed. International Critical Commentary. Edinburgh: T & T Clark, 1902.

Sanders, Jack T. *New Testament Ethics*. Philadelphia: Fortress Press, 1975.

Scanzoni, Letha, and Virginia A. Mollenkott. *Is the Homosexual My Neigh-bor?* San Francisco: Harper & Row, 1978.

Schlier, Heinrich. *Der Römerbrief.* Herders theologischer Kommentar zum Neuen Testament. Freiburg: Herder, 1977.

Schmithals, Walter. *An Introduction to the Theology of Rudolf Bultmann.* Trans. John Bowden. Minneapolis: Augsburg, 1968.

———. *Gnosticism in Corinth.* Trans. John E. Steeley. Nashville: Abingdon Press, 1971.

———. *Der Römerbrief als historisches Problem.* Studien zum Neuen Testament 9. Gütersloh: Gerd Mohn, 1975.

Schoeps, Hans-Joachim. "Überlegungen zum Problem der Homo-sexualität." *Der homosexuelle Nächste*. Ed. Hermanus Bianchi u.a. Hamburg: Furche, 1963. Pp. 74–114.

Scroggs, Robin. *The New Testament and Homosexuality*. Philadelphia: Fortress Press, 1983.

Segundo, Juan Luis. *The Liberation of Theology*. Trans. John Drury. Maryknoll, NY: Orbis Books, 1976.

Shafer, Byron E. "The Church and Homosexuality." *Minutes of the General Assembly of the United Presbyterian Church in the USA*. Part 1, Journal. New York: Office of the General Assembly of the United Presbyterian Church in the USA. November 1978. Pp. 213–60.

Simpson, William K. *The Literature of Ancient Egypt*. New ed. New Haven, CT: Yale University Press, 1973.

Snaith, Norman, ed. *Leviticus and Numbers*. The Century Bible. Nashville: Thomas Nelson, 1967.

Soggin, J. Alberto. *Judges.* Trans. John Bowden. Old Testament Library. Philadelphia: Westminster Press, 1981.

Spitzer, Robert L. "A Proposal About Homosexuality and the APA Nomenclature: Homosexuality as One Form of Sexual Behavior and Sexual Orientation Disturbance as a Psychiatric Disorder." A paper attached to a press release of the American Psychiatric Association, 1700 18th St., NW, Washington, DC 20009, December 15, 1973.

Stendahl, Krister. "Biblical Theology, Contemporary." In *Interpreter's Dictionary of the Bible.* Ed. G.A. Buttrick and others. Nashville: Abingdon Press, 1962. Vol. A–D:418–32.

Strabo. *Geography.* 5 vols. Trans. H.L. Jones. Loeb Classical Library. Cambridge, MA: Harvard University Press, 1928.

Symonds, John Addington. *A Problem in Modern Ethics.* London: n.p., 1891.

Thomas, D. Winton. "*KELEBH* 'Dog': Its Origin and Some Usages of It in the Old Testament." *Vetus Testamentum* 10 (1960):423–26.

Thompson, Thomas L. *The Historicity of the Patriarchal Narratives.* Beiheft zu Zeitschrift für die alttestamentliche Wissenschaft 133. New York: Walter de Gruyter, 1974.

Tillich, Paul. *Systematic Theology.* Vol. 2. Chicago: University of Chicago, 1962.

Vanggaard, Thorkil. *Phallós: A Symbol and Its History in the Male World.* Trans. Thorkil Vanggaard. London: Jonathan Cape, 1972.

Via, Dan O. *Kerygma and Comedy in the New Testament.* Philadelphia: Fortress Press, 1975.

———. *The Parables.* Philadelphia: Fortress Press, 1967.

Wallis, Gerhard. See Bergman, Jan.

Ward, James M. *Amos and Isaiah.* Nashville: Abingdon Press, 1969.

Weeks, Jeffrey. *Coming Out.* New York: Quartet, 1977.

Weinberg, George. *Society and the Healthy Homosexual.* New York: St. Martin's Press, 1972.

Weinberg, Martin S., and Colin J. Williams. *Male Homosexuals: Their Problems and Adaptations.* New York: Oxford University Press, 1974.

Weiser, Artur. *Das Buch der zwölf kleinen Propheten.* Bd. 1. 6. Aufl. Alte Testament Deutsch. Göttingen: Vandenhoeck & Ruprecht, 1974.

Weiss, Carl, and David J. Friar. *Terror in the Prisons.* Indianapolis: Bobbs-Merrill, 1974.

Whale, John. "Leviticus Revisited." *Sunday Times.* London. November 21, 1982.

Whiston, William, trans. *The Works of Flavius Josephus.* Vol. 1. Philadelphia: J. Grigg, 1831.

Whitaker, Richard E. *A Concordance of Ugaritic Literature.* Cambridge, MA: Harvard University Press, 1972.

Williams, Daniel Day. "Love." *Handbook of Christian Theology*. Ed. Marvin Halverson and Arthur Cohen. New York: Meridian, 1958. Pp. 216–20.

——. *The Spirit and the Forms of Love*. New York: Harper & Row, 1968.

Wink, Walter. *The Bible in Human Transformation*. Philadelphia: Fortress Press, 1973.

Wissowa, Georg, und Wilhelm Kroll, Hrsg. *Paulys Realencyclopaedia der classischen Altertumwissenschaft*. 73 vols. Stuttgart: J.B. Metzler, 1921–68.

Wolfenden, John, chpsn. *The Wolfenden Report*. Introduction by Karl Menninger. New York: Stein & Day, 1963.

Wuellner, Wilhelm. "Paul's Rhetoric of Argumentation in Romans." *Catholic Biblical Quarterly* 38 (1976):330–51.

INDEX

Justice (*see* Righteousness)
Justificatio impii 87
Justification by faith 11, 76
Justinian 25, 29, 63
Juvenis (young man) 30

K

Käsemann, E. 12, 71, 87–88, 93, 107–9, 124
Kamlah, E. 90
Kaposi's Sarcoma 117
Katchadourian, H.A. 80, 85, 116
Keck, L.E. 69
Keil, C.F. 64
Kelebh (dog) 61
Kertbeny, K.M (*see* Benkert)
Kinaidos (catamite) 56, 83
King, M.L., Jr. 127–28
King James Version 15, 54, 62
1 Kings
    1:4   32
    11:7   64
    12:25–33   60
    14:24   42, 54, 57, 61, 64, 68
    15:12   42, 57, 61, 64, 68
    22:46   42, 57, 61, 64
1 and 2 Kings   48
2 Kings
    21:1–18   63
    22:8   59
    23   63
    23:7   42, 55, 61, 64, 68
    23:9   61
    23:26   63
Kinsey, A.C. 17–18, 22–24, 117, 125
Klostermann, A. 65
Knabenliebe (pederasty) 29
Knabenschänderei (child molestation) 29, 82
Knabenschändung 29
Krafft-Ebing, R. 14, 29
Kroll, W. 29
Kropotkin, P.A. 10
Kümmel, W.G. 75, 97, 102, 108

L

Lamentations 4:6   48, 50
Lang, D. 78
Lara-Braud, J. 3
Laughton, C. 117
Legal rectitude 76–77, 97–101, 106
Leprosy 14–16
Lesbian(-ism) 20, 22, 26, 77, 85, 89, 100, 113, 125–27 (*see also* Homosexual, Gay/lesbian liberation)
Leviticus   52, 66–67
    11:7f.   65
    13:2–46   15
    15:2–15   63
    17—26   47
    18   65–66
    18:5   11
    18:21   65
    18:22   28, 52, 54, 58, 61, 64–65, 68, 71, 90
    18:23   66
    18:26–27,29–30   65
    19:2   65
    19:18   105, 112
    19:30   65
    20   65–66
    20:7,26   65
    20:13   52, 54, 58, 61, 64, 68, 71, 90
    20:13,23   28
    20:15–16   66
Lewis, Bill, 118
Lewis, C.T. 30
Liberation theology 50, 68–69, 77, 124, 126
    defined 27
    and development 4, 127
    liberationist hermeneutic 6, 51, 64–69, 77, 100–101
    as new approach to Bible 4
    no orthodox version 9
    as related to gay liberation 3–23
Lieberson, J. 118
Lietzmann, H. 93
Lindemann, A. 102

F

l